BRITAIN AND FRANCE, THE UNRULY TWINS

BRITAIN AND FRANCE,
THE UNRULY TWINS

by

JOSEPH CHIARI
Docteur ès Lettres

VISION

Vision Press Limited
157 Knightsbridge
London, S.W.1

SBN 85478 202 8

89329

Printed in Great Britain
by Clarke, Doble & Brendon Ltd., Plymouth

MCMLXXI

Contents

Foreword

In this fascinating book my friend Dr. Chiari traces the extraordinary history of England, France and Scotland with rare lucidity. I say rare, because the story itself is entangled and entwined to a point at which, to the lay reader, it often becomes incomprehensible. Wars, friendships, occupations and dynastic rivalries, followed each other with bewildering rapidity. Geographically and culturally these countries could never be kept apart from one another; while, from the religious and political points of view, bitter strife prevailed over long periods of time between them. The basic theme that emerges from Dr. Chiari's book is that whenever they fought each other, as they did almost endlessly, Europe, and a world then dominated by Europe, stood poised upon the brink of destruction; whereas, on the rare occasions, such as the nineteenth century, when friendship gained the upper hand, another European *renaissance*, always waiting to blossom, burst out in its full glory.

Dr. Chiari picks up all the complex threads—political, philosophical, religious, poetic—and weaves them into a comprehensive whole. His book should be read by all those who believe, as I do, that the only hope of a genuine European *renaissance* in the modern world, lies in a revival of the *Entente Cordiale*.

Boothby.

House of Lords,
Westminster.

I

History—Generalities

Strictest judge of her own worth, gentlest of man's mind,
First to follow Truth and last to leave old Truths behind—
France, beloved of every soul that loves its fellow-kind!

Ere our birth (rememberest thou?) side by side we lay
Fretting in the womb of Rome to begin our fray.
Ere men knew our tongues apart, our one task was known—
Each to mould the other's fate as he wrought his own.
To this end we stirred mankind till all Earth was ours,
Till our world-end strifes begat wayside Thrones and Powers—
Puppets that we made or broke to bar the other's path—
Necessary, outpost-folk, hirelings of our wrath.
To this end we stormed the seas, tack for tack, and burst
Through the doorways of new worlds, doubtful which was first,
Hand on hilt (rememberest thou?) ready for the blow—
Sure, whatever else we met, we should meet our foe.
Spurred or balked at every stride by the other's strength,
So we rode the ages down and every ocean's length! *

Thus Kipling, and how right he was! France and England
have fought for centuries on all the battlefields of the world. That
is the truth; but so have, for centuries, English and Scots, Irish
and English, and yet they now live as one great family, not so
much because they speak the same language, but because they
share similar ideals and because through war and peace they
have each absorbed some of the other's characteristics. The wars
which divided these nations were family wars; they fought each
other, in the same way as Armagnacs fought Burgundians, who
fought against the French on the side of the English, while the

* Rudyard Kipling, *France 1913.*

Scots were, for over three centuries, on the side of the French, and this, both for dynastic and interested reasons, and also because, although members of the same family, there were and there still are more affinities and similarities of character between the Scots and the French than between the French and the English or, to a large extent, between the English and the Scots. This last point is an important element in the Franco-British partnership in which Scotland stands as one of the key links in the similarity of ideals and common aims existing between Britain and France.

The wars in which England, Scotland and France were involved between the end of the fourteenth century and the beginning of the sixteenth were dynastic, feudal and professional wars for territorial aggrandizements, but without any nationalistic feelings or animosity involved in them. That does not mean that they were exempt from sheer violence and brutality. When William Wallace was at last defeated and caught by the English, he was dismembered and beheaded. Such deeds were part and parcel of rough medieval justice, which admitted the cutting off of hands and fingers, and even the gouging out of eyes, as a punishment for various misdeeds in which relevant parts of the human anatomy had been involved. We were still living in the age of *Le jugement de Dieu*, which consisted in the fact that the one who was defeated was necessarily guilty. But this did not prevent respect for the rules of the game of war, and these rules were, on the whole, scrupulously observed. Enemies who surrendered were spared, and they could, of course, be ransomed. Besides that, the royal families of these three countries were closely interrelated, and so were many of their nobles who fought at their sides. Henry VIII and Francis I could meet and indulge in festivities and jousting at the Field of the Cloth of Gold before going each their separate way towards the battlefield. Henry Curtmantle and Richard the Lion-heart were French princes, both buried in France, and they and their successors claimed the throne of France for the same reasons that the French Kings claimed the throne of England, or the English the throne of Scotland.

Without the help of the Scots, Joan of Arc's generalship would not have succeeded in "throwing the English out of France", and she wanted to do that, not because she hated them, but because the English should, according to her, stay in their own land.

In the name of an alliance which was supposed to go back to Charlemagne, the Scots kept on sending to France forces which they could ill afford to spare and which paid dearly for the final defeat of the English in France. Orleans would not have been taken and Charles VII would never have been crowned King without their help. Once that was done, the Scots having been severely depleted in the process, Joan of Arc was burnt at Rouen by a subtle combination of English military might and French churchmen, who found her claim of direct conversations with God and with her angels as preposterous as English war leaders had found her generalship and defeat at her hands unacceptable. Less than a hundred years later, again following the call of a French King, the King of Scotland, the unlucky James IV, encountered at Flodden, at the hands of the English, a defeat from which the House of Stuart never recovered. There "the flowers of the forest" were all laid to rest and the death knell, which was heard on the battlefield of Flodden, was later echoed by the dull thud of the axe which fell on the most tragic member of the Stuart family at Fotheringay Castle in January 1587. After the death of Francis I, England is in the ascendancy, and France, torn by the wars of religion, will not take again the field against England until the age of Louis XIV, when brilliant generals like the Duke of Marlborough and Turenne handled armies like master chess-players. A few years later, the battle of Fontenoy epitomizes the type of spirit, at its best, which prevailed in the wars between Britain and France. There, French and English troops, barely fifty yards apart, suddenly came to a halt and their respective officers doffed their hats and politely entreated each other to fire first. "No, no, after you." "No, after you!" After much parleying, the English were prevailed upon to do the French the honour of firing first, and so they did, gallantly wiping out the first line with their first volley. Those were the days! When later on French and English troops met in far-away parts of the globe, in Canada and in India, they showed the same professionalism and respect for conventions in wars which were carried out by soldiers, who, like Montcalm, were prepared to die for what their disdainful masters, engrossed in the gay, factitious life of Versailles, described as a few acres of snow-covered lands.

During the Revolution and the Napoleonic wars, London is

11

teeming with French *émigrés*, whose presence gives a flavour of civil war to the struggle between France and her opponents. But in England, as well as in Scotland, the Revolution and Napoleon had their allies. Napoleon, who was both a romantic at heart and also the typical romantic hero, if ever there was one, was so much under the spell of Ossian's poetry that, for a long time, he carried constantly a volume of his poems in his pocket. The great romantic poets, Burns, Shelley, Wordsworth and Byron, were full of admiration for him, and Carlyle saw in him the archetype of the heroic character. Napoleon himself was not without affinities for the English, and it is not without reason that, once he was defeated, he chose to surrender to the English, with the hope of rejoining his brother Lucien, who was already living in England. When he arrived in the Bay of Plymouth, on his way to his unfortunate island of St. Helena, he was nearly mobbed by the people, who realized, as soon as they saw him or met him, that he was no ogre, but on the contrary a likeable and friendly human being who had come to ask for a place of rest at the hearth of his former enemies. During the time when he was at war with England, the artistic and scientific exchanges between the two countries were not interrupted, and French dandies still had their linen laundered in London, while many of Napoleon's soldiers tramped across Europe in English boots, for English boots were the best. Even when he was at St. Helena, confronted with the total lack of comprehension of Sir Hudson Lowe, Napoleon kept on hoping that the Whigs and the Prince Regent, upon whom he had pinned his faith, would some day bring him back to Europe. Who knows what dreams went on in his Promethean head? He perhaps remembered that, but for a freak of fate, he might have been born an Englishman! For such were the desires of Corsicans in the seventeen sixties, when, encouraged by Rousseau and James Burrell, they were fighting against the Genoese and their successors, the French, for their independence. How strange that it was side by side with Corsicans, fighting against the French, that Nelson lost his eye in front of Calvi. Did he think of Calvi when, with his telescope to his right eye, he watched the arrow of his ships bearing down on the French and Spanish line at Trafalgar? Years before, on the 8th of May 1769, three months before Napoleon was born, his nationality was decided on the battlefield of Ponte Novo, where Pascal

Paoli, the leader of the Corsicans, whose bust is in Westminster Abbey, was defeated by the French. Napoleon was thus born under the French flag. So the die was cast, and the shots which put an end to Corsica's dream of independence heralded the opening of an age of turmoil and wars, which only came to an end when the curtain fell at last at Waterloo.

Waterloo marked the end of the wars between England and France, and it is worth remembering that at Waterloo there were Scots on both sides. The illustrious Scot, Marshall MacDonald, was not the only one on Napoleon's side. Since the days of the famous "Garde Ecossaise" of French monarchs, the Scots in France, whose number had been swelled by the exiles of 1745, had always played a lively part in French arms. Since this famous last battle, France and England have been side by side in the defence of the same ideals, the first and foremost of which is the respect of individual freedom. France and Britain are old nations, the oldest in Europe; they were already nations when the rest of Europe was still divided into warring factions and principalities. Russia began with Peter the Great, Germany and Italy were only welded into nations in the last quarter of the nineteenth century, and Spain and Portugal, after having built great colonial empires, sank into exhaustion. While all these countries were still practically non-existent as nations and were torn by feudal anarchy, France, England and Scotland were already evolved enough to be able to indulge the luxury of dynastic wars, and, by the thirteenth century, the Arbroath Declaration, and Magna Carta, and, at the beginning of the fourteenth century, the General Estates of Paris, had already made clear the fact that as far as these countries were concerned authority had to rest on consent and not simply on brute force. These were the beginnings of democracy and of constitutional monarchy, and Calvinism and Protestantism in due time helped to spread these notions in France as well as in England and Scotland.

The Scots, who are the linch-pin between England and France, responded eagerly to Calvinism, which gave moral and religious support to the democratic principles of the Declaration of Arbroath, and to the love of equalitarianism which, as in the case of the French, is part of their make-up. The clan system was not a feudal system, but a family-like organization with various

13

attributes and responsibilities in which all the component members were nominally equal. The chief of the clan treated the members of his clan as fellow human beings. Burns, who sums up so admirably the Scottish ethos, expressed this notion at its best in the famous words "A man's a man for a' that". Imbued with humanitarianism and with the love of freedom, longing also perhaps for lost national independence, Burns eagerly welcomed the motto and the spirit of the French Revolution, and so did many of his fellow Scots. A society, *Les Amis du Peuple*, was founded in Edinburgh, and the equalitarian Scots welcomed the end of social inequalities and privileges in France. Burns's satirical poetry is as biting as the drawings of Daumier or of Hogarth, and it shows the same savage indignation at the suffering of the poor. Byron, like Burns, cannot be understood or fully appreciated without the context and the spiritual climate of his native land. His passionate temperament, his intellectual curiosity, his interest in mental speculations, his self-irony and mockery, are typically Scots, as Scots as the romanticism of Ossian or of Walter Scott, who, like Byron, held Europe under his spell for a time. The whole of the historical novel in France is indebted to him. Listening to Hugo reading one of his novels, Vigny said: "I seem to be listening to Walter Scott." Vigny himself imitated Scott in *Cinq-Mars*, and Balzac held him in great admiration. "Compared with him," he said, "Byron is nothing or practically nothing. . . . Scott will go on rising, while Byron will fall." Dumas had the same reverence for him, and he said that one ought to imitate Scott as Raphael imitated Il Perugino. Mérimée's masterpiece *Colomba* is, up to a point, an imitation of Scott's dramatic skills and presentation of characters. George Sand said: "Scott's novels inspire me with courage and lift me above myself." These are tributes of serious and important writers, who, whatever they may have learnt or derived from Scott, show clearly the reverence in which he was held and the influence he had on French Romanticism.*

Before the full blossom of Romanticism, David Hume, who spoke and wrote French fluently, had already shown evidence of the affinities between the Scots and the French in philosophy. Hume's introspective empiricism and scepticism certainly fostered

* In our time, G. Lukacs looks upon him as the father of the historical novel and of social realism.

the growth of unreason, which, from Rousseau to Schopenhauer, Kierkegaard, Nietzsche and Bergson, has affected the nineteenth century, particularly in its closing stages, and the beginning of the twentieth.

From the point of view of character, the Scots are less reserved than the English; they are more curious about people and countries, more interested in intellectual pursuits, logic, clarity of thought and expression, and in sheer hard common sense. The English do not lack common sense, but they can, more than the Scots or the French, be swayed or motivated by sentiment. The Scots are in these various respects, quite close to the French; yet they are also very close to the English in having a strong religious sense and in having evolved, like them, a morality which has, on the whole, a religious foundation. The intellectual curiosity and scepticism of the Scots, which encourages psychology and the study of man, rarely leads to the kind of metaphysical speculation that either questions the existence of God or replaces the idea of God by pure metaphysics. Their strong moral sense makes them shun both materialism and pure idealism, being in this respect disciples of Hume, who stands half-way between Locke's empiricism and Descartes' scepticism and Kantian idealism.

Modern Scotland, with its aspirations towards certain definite aspects of nationhood, its liberal attitude towards people of different races and creeds, its internationalism, continues to display, in the arts and in poetry, some of the well known traits of its genius. Nobody exhibits these better than Hugh MacDiarmid, who is a poet of European stature and possibly the best poet Scotland has yet produced. With him we find again the blend of passion and intellect, the burning concern for social and human problems, the biting satire, the love of independence and the lyrical purity which mark the poetry of Burns, together with a greater intellectual power which enables him to lift poetry to metaphysical explorations.

15

II

Characters and Attitudes

"Whenever I hear the word culture," Goering was supposed to
have said, "I reach for my revolver."* The French certainly do
not do that. They might, at the most, reach for *Larousse*; yet
they are more likely to fall into the ecstasy of a dream which will
toss them about from the shores of Greece, the mother of culture,
to the music of the names adorning their streets, or they will hold
conversations with the great shades which haunt the Pantheon.
The French, to be sure, take culture seriously, and if Victor Hugo
was, according to Cocteau, *"un poète qui se prenait pour Victor
Hugo"*, many a budding culture-maker in France sees himself, if
not as a Victor Hugo, Baudelaire or Rimbaud, at least as the
bearer of a name which will perhaps one day be carved at the
entrance of broad avenues, from where it might dazzle countless
generations of onlookers. The English hold less exalted views
about culture. They do not quite join Malherbe in saying that *"un
bon poète n'est pas plus utile à l'état qu'un bon joueur de quilles"*,
but they might very well replace *"quilles"* by cricket, for cricket
is more exalted, nobler than skittles, and if a poet like John Betjeman can both practise verse and praise cricket, tennis and country
life, then the whole English world lies all before him. To be true,
I am very glad of this, for I admire a great deal of John Betjeman's
poetry and there is not a better cicerone in the world with whom
to visit places of beauty and historical interest. He is a great
success because his love of nature and of places of beauty, his interest in people, his quiet humour and his mixture of whimsicality
and seriousness, which lacks neither sincerity nor a certain depth,
without ever being stuffy, admirably reflect the English ethos. The

---

* He had been anticipated by one of his fellow countrymen, the writer
Hans Gohst, who in 1934 said in one of his plays: "Whenever I hear the
word culture, I release the safety-catch of my revolver."

16

French poet is not expected to praise or to play cricket. He can, like Baudelaire, dream of the barricades, where he could perhaps shoot or watch the shooting of some General Aupick whom he dislikes, but his main task is not to praise but to warn, to reveal truth as he sees it, and to play a professional part in a society which, if pleased with him, could reward him with ribbons, professorial chairs and street names or a green uniform.

Until recently, the French had a Minister of Culture, M. Malraux, who is himself one of the foremost creative minds of our age. The English had, at the same time, a Minister of the Arts, a very distinguished and praiseworthy lady, Miss Jennie Lee, who has done a great deal for the arts in this country. Both the description of the office and the respective professions of the occupants imply a different approach to the problem of culture, to art and to the very ethos of the artist. It is something which could be described as a kind of professionalism on the one side and a kind of amateurism on the other. The French developed very early a high regard for the artist and for the creative mind, in whatever medium it may work. Even their metaphysical thought, from Descartes to Bergson, partakes of aesthetics. Nietzsche was probably thinking of French art when he wrote: "the beautiful is the mirror of the logical, that is to say, the laws of logic are the object of the laws of the beautiful." No nation, in spite of a few exceptions like those of the German states which held Leibnitz, Goethe and Hegel in high regard, has shown greater respect than France for the products of the mind and for their authors. Where else but in France could one find a small provincial town like Calais boasting of a *Rue Homère*, a *Rue Ovide*, a *Rue Horace* and a *Rue Pindare*, and all these streets intersecting the *Rue Victor Hugo?* Victor Hugo's name is everywhere, including, of course, Paris, where one of its main avenues is dedicated to him. This distribution of writers' names to streets is not done at random; far from it; it is something as orderly as a history of literature or of the arts, or of history itself. When in the enchanting Roman town of Nîmes you encounter *la Rue Paul Valéry*, you expect, and you find near it, *la Rue Paul Verlaine* and *la Rue Arthur Rimbaud*. How pleasant it would be to be able to move from Shakespeare's to Marlowe's or Ben Jonson's Avenue or from Blake's Place to Burns's Street or Coleridge Avenue! This will probably come, but not yet.

The French have had a long innings and, although no fiddle-player has been the ruler of France, as Nero was of Rome, many of their most exalted political figures and civil servants have been men of letters. Brantôme and Ronsard were French Ambassadors in Scotland. Du Bellay was a secretary in the French Embassy in Rome. Racine and Boileau were Louis XIV's historiographers. Voltaire was an ambassador at large to the court of Frederick of Prussia and to that of Catherine the Great. Lamartine was president of the Chamber of Deputies and a Minister; Chateaubriand was Minister for Foreign Affairs and Ambassador of France in Rome. Stendhal was Vice-Consul in Milan and, as such, the despair of the Ministry, for he was more often in Rome than at his post. Claudel was an Ambassador; St. John Perse was permanent secretary of the French Foreign Office; Giraudoux was an Inspector of Diplomatic and Consular Posts and M. Malraux who was Minister of Information became Minister of Culture.

In England, men of letters never cut much of a figure in political life. One single, magnificent exception—Francis Bacon, Lord Chancellor of England in the age of Shakespeare, an age in which, if poets had been granted the reverence which they deserved, Shakespeare would duly have been elected Emperor of the West. Plato, who ought to have known better, since he was himself no mean poet, could only picture the poet in the throes of inspiration and listening to the voice of the Muse and not to that of Reason; so he banished him from his city. Yet what better and wiser ruler could the world have ever had than the poet, who, through Prospero's Magic, could use the violence of sea-storms and shipwrecks, not to wound or to cause suffering, but simply to redress rights and restore justice! *There* was the hand that could rule chaos and extract from it the very peace and justice of heaven! With the exception of Christ's outstretched arms upon the Cross, no mere man could dream of doing better.

The French state, whether it was a monarchy, an empire or a republic, probably very much aware of the popular will on this subject, seems to have taken a constant interest in what is generally called culture. Eleanor of Aquitaine with her brilliant court, and the two Marguerites, Marguerite Queen of Navarre, and Marguerite of Valois, Queen of France, were all poets and patrons of the arts and of artists. The French Kings have been throughout the patrons of the Sorbonne, and by 1635, Richelieu, the ruler of the day, founded the Academy. A few years later came the *Comédie Française*, the importance of which did not escape Napoleon, even when he was in snow-bound, smouldering Moscow. England founded in 1660 the Royal Society of Science, which preceded by six years the creation of *L'Académie des Sciences*. That was, and is, a much revered institution, yet, all in all, there is nothing in this country which compares with the large number of Academies and prizes of all sorts which, in France, can be awarded to artists. Whether this is good or bad is a debatable point. What matters is that, without ignoring the purely commercial interests which underlie many of these enterprises, they do testify to a very lively and conscious interest in the arts.

Consciousness is certainly one of the dominant traits of French art and of the French genius. To know what one does, and not to learn through what one is doing or about what one is trying to do, is an attitude which underlies many aspects of French activities and differentiates them from the fundamental English approach which is to do things and to learn in the process, and, side by side with this pragmatism, to trust in the power of imagination to give to "airy nothings a habitation and a name", or to perceive under the appearances, as Wordsworth put it, the tremble of true reality. These revelations are only possible if one allows the imagination to carry out its visions and its syntheses, without the interference of rational glasses or deforming prisms. Valéry said that he preferred a few words written in a state of full consciousness to a page written under the dictation of inspiration. Everyone dislikes dictation, even if it is done under the guidance of inspiration. Yet this is, of course, a concept without any real foundation, except in the legendary days of Gods and Goddesses, of whispering oak leaves and smoke-wrapped tripods upon which sat Cassandra or other mouthpieces of the Gods. When St. Augustine, strolling in his garden, heard a voice say "take and read", he obeyed; so did Joan of Arc when she heard the voices of St. Michael and St. Catherine under the oak trees of Lorraine. St. John of the Cross, in his *Noce oscura*, did the same, and so did many famous saints whom God either took by the hand or to whom He showed light in thick darkness and rich blossoms in deserts. Inspiration in the arts is something similar: it is the glory and the dream of Wordsworth, the Blakean capacity to see "the universe in a grain of sand", or Herrick's vision of "Eternity in a ring of light". No one dictates such visions. On the contrary, the poet, by some kind of ascesis, sheds off his scales of intellect, prejudice and age, and, going back to the dawn of his life, which is also essential, eternal life, he connects with, registers and records the visions and the intimations from a timeless world. When he carries out such an operation, he is not in a state of divagation. He is in a state of receptivity, a state in which, disconnected from the perceptual world, his essential self, which links him with individuated essences, unfolds, through words, the experience of intensely lived moments. These fuse together past and present into the organic entity of the poem, which has, once it is completed, a life of its own. Fused at intense heat, from substances which are part of the inner being of the poet, who, when he writes, is nothing but the poem itself, these experiences are the revelations of truths which, as Hopkins put it, human nature receives "with a shock and a tremble". As we shall see later, most late nineteenth century French writers shared this approach to art, which, on the whole, is no more basic to French genius than that which consists in becoming, and knowing, through doing things.

The French, Celtic in this respect, are at the same time both explorers of, and sticklers for, forms and styles. The English, on the other hand, seem to subscribe more to the Coleridgean notion that "No work of genius could want its form". Very early in their history, the French explored and established most of the verse forms which later were widely adopted by the rest of Europe. Yet this deep respect for form can also act as blinkers which prevent one from ever swerving away from the all too well ploughed furrow.

Art admittedly requires rules; if not, it turns into anarchy or the pure subjectivism of action painting, which is no doubt probably therapeutic, but hardly conducive to experiences which can communicate themselves to onlookers. The English are not generally given to pure subjectivity, to wearing their hearts on their sleeves or to parading about in the nude. The French have had their moments of wearing their hearts on their sleeves, during the Romantic age, and their moments of unbridled subjectivity, during the surrealist twenties, which, again, as far as surrealist

20

theory is concerned, was more a therapeutic phase than a great creative phase. For indeed, although it produced some worthwhile results in painting, it certainly did not produce any poetry worth talking about. It is safe to say that the very basis of surrealism, the rejection of reason and the total trust in the value of the subconscious, are not attitudes native to the French genius. In fact, it can be said that every one of its aspects is definitely against it. Misty intoxication with dreams, with the subconscious, or with vague legends would, on the whole, as far as France is concerned, be laughed out of court. These notions would easily be dispelled and dissolved by the laughter of Rabelais, Molière, La Fontaine, Voltaire and Beaumarchais, and by the scepticism of Montaigne and Descartes, both laughter and scepticism militating in favour of sobriety, a strong sense of human limitations and of the widely accepted notion that ridicule is the best weapon to deflate pomposity and human pretences. Daumier's satires, Paul-Louis Courier's pamphlets were more effective correctives to morals than church sermons. Besides that, there is the fact that the well known love of form of the French cannot be reconciled with the haphazard compositions or, should one say, gratuitous outbursts, of surrealism. One has only to think of Pascal apologizing for the fact that he could not make the eighteenth *Provinciale* short enough, because he did not have enough time to do so, or of Flaubert at grips with *les affres du style*, to realize how alien this notion is to the French mind, much preoccupied with consciousness in art.

The rationalism which is the basis of faith in consciousness, control in art, scepticism and avoidance of extremes in moral attitudes and in social life, is also the root of the well known French irreverence for authority, religious or profane, and for superstition and mystery. The French seem to show an extreme attachment to the word "free". They claim to love freedom, to be free-thinkers, and to be free from inhibiting moral conventions. They forget, of course, the fanaticism of the religious wars and that of the Revolution, although they might excuse themselves by echoing Pascal, who said that he only believed in ideas for which men were prepared to die. They forget also the extraordinary stuffiness of convention-ridden French provincial life, which was a kind of Abbaye de Thélème compared with life in Victorian

England. Freedom from intolerance and superstition was the battlecry of the eighteenth century philosophers, and libertinism pervaded French society from the seventeenth century onwards. As for anticlericalism, it is a typically French phenomenon, and it remains one of the two stock attitudes of the parties of the left, the other being a kind of undying chameleon-like Jacobinism, which leads every one of these parties to claim the title of being the true and only heir of the great Revolution. Thence the fixation upon the notion of revolutionary violence of these parties, who misguidedly claim Marx as their father, irrespective of the fact that the latter has clearly pointed out that such an attitude can only lead to barren political power. "Any revolution of the proletariat trying to create politically conditions not yet developed in the socio-economic field is doomed to failure . . . our party can only achieve power if and when conditions permit to realize its own views."* This Marxist point of view goes a long way to explain the reaction of the French Communist Party towards what Marx would have described as *les enragés* or *les émeutiers* of the madness in Paris in May 1968.

The English are not irreverent; they are, on the other hand, humorous, and their humour is different from the French, in the same sense that French humour is mostly directed against institutions, attitudes and behaviour, in a sometimes dehumanized and destructive way. French humour shares with the Scots and the Irish, who are irreverent towards clerics, a strong taste for the macabre. English humour generally respects institutions; it is directed at human behaviour, attitudes and situations, and it is, on the whole, humane and rarely uncharitable, so much so, for instance, that an Irish playwright like Brendan Behan can be sufficiently anglicized to show, in his play *The Hostage*, that he can poke fun at the English without being uncharitable, even in a revolutionary situation.

The English are great believers in spontaneity and sincerity in art, that is to say, they believe in "the true voice of feeling", and in the poet warbling his musical notes with the same naturalness as a bird pouring out its song. This does not mean, of course, expressionism, which they shun as vulgar and exhibitionist; it means, on the contrary, a careful avoidance of conceptualism and rhetoric

* Marx, *Werke*, IX, 514 f.

22

in art, which, according to them, ought to be both organic, that is to say, involving the whole being, and impersonal, in the sense that it is universal and is valid for all men.

The French are probably more than any other people concerned with universality and objectivity in art. On the other hand, organicity, though playing an important part in French art, particularly in pre-Renaissance and in nineteenth century and twentieth century art, is seriously counteracted by conceptualism and intellectualism.

"Le génie est une longue patience", said Buffon, and Racine, writing to a friend, said: "My tragedy is finished; nothing remains but to write it." This is certainly a conceptual approach to art, worthy of a people who prize intellect and order above all things. A French park is not an English common; in the one, everything is order, calm and, perhaps, joy, for those who like it that way. In the other, it is the naturalness, the organic development of things, that matters and pleases. Racine reduced his tragedies to an essential coherence of plot and character, embodied in a style which is basically functional, that is, shorn of images and metaphors, and so is all the more charged with dramatic intensity as it is simple and direct, in situations which imply and carry extraordinary tensions. Shakespeare's world is, on the contrary, cosmic. He always deals both with particular individuals and with archetypes who rise to the level of the human condition and therefore embrace practically every one of its important aspects. His language is both dramatic and rich in metaphors and images which give the whole a transcendental aura relating the human to the Eternal. Yet, if Boileau advocates conceptualism, and Racine pares tragedy to what he thinks is essential, Rabelais, Hugo and Claudel shun conceptualism and schematizations and grapple with the whole of life, with the high and the low, the comic and the tragic, the small and the enormous, all interlocked in the same works which, if one adopted rigid attitudes, could be said not to belong to a so-called great French tradition, if ever there were such a thing as one main tradition. For, if it came to that, where should one place French symbolism, which, as we shall see later, although it has typically French traits, is closely connected with English Romanticism, and also expresses, more than anything else, the Celtic element of the French genius? Therefore, although one may point out what seem

to be dominant traits of a given art, it is evident that one cannot hope to enclose the art of any nation within clearcut categories.

English art is more concerned with morality and utilitarianism than French art; it has to be since morality, at least social morality, plays a much more important part in England than in France. Here two simple and everyday aphorisms, framed in different terms yet expressing similar ideas, seem to illustrate and to make clear certain vital aspects of the English and the French character. When an Englishman is in trouble, he endeavours to keep a stiff upper lip. When a Frenchman is in trouble, he is not concerned with his stiff or trembling upper lip, he is concerned with another part of his anatomy, *il serre les fesses*. The images used, and the anatomical parts involved, are a revealing illustration of the psychology of the English and of the French. The Englishman, when in trouble, is concerned, above all, with appearances and decorum; he must not show any signs of fear or distress, whatever he may feel inside himself. This is obviously part of the banishment, or the control, of the emotions, which, since the establishment of the public school system in England, has been one of the basic tenets of English education. The Frenchman, on the other hand, is concerned not with appearances and decorum but with a biological fact which consists in avoiding a possibly disastrous relaxation of muscular tension. The Englishman is in fact concerned with the moral aspect of the situation and with the image which others will have of him; the Frenchman is concerned with stark reality, which, in the end, may only be known to himself alone but is nevertheless what matters to him. He is concerned with his self-respect in a purely personal context and not as defined by others. With the English, it is, as with the Japanese and the Chinese, a question of face; with the French, it is a question of pride, that is to say, of what the individual thinks and not what other people think about him. These conclusions lead straight to the well known individualism of the French and to the group and social consciousness of the English. I have been stuck in a snow-drift in France and I have watched with dismay twenty cars pass by at speed without the driver of any one of them even murmuring a word of encouragement. The car, the snow, the getting out of it, was all my own business. In England, practically every passing car would have stopped, and with a great heave of communal effort, we would have pulled the car out of the snow and moved off in procession. Individualism, yes, but in cases of snow-drifts, England any time!

When the Englishman wants to convey the notion that one should not attempt to do what one cannot do, he says: "one must not bite off more than one can chew." The Frenchman might endeavour to convey the same or some similar idea with the expression: *"il faut savoir reconnaître ses possibilités"* or words to that effect; but if one can afford to speak naturally, without frills, he is more likely to say: *"il ne faut pas essayer de péter plus haut que son derrière"*, an aphorism which, though earthy, is both most appropriate to the thought to be conveyed and also very expressive of the French make-up. The English aphorism carries both an element of moral judgement and a suggestion that, through experience, one could learn, in the end, to bite off just what one can chew, and no more. This is a notion perfectly in keeping with the English character, which relies on experimentalism as the basis of knowledge and on control of the will as the basis of morality. The Rabelaisian* connotations of the French aphorism, on the other hand, are very much in keeping with the French character. First of all, the French, although not experimentalist, are realist, in the philosophical meaning of the word: realism consisting in looking upon any aspect of reality as informed with essence and value and as an integral part of the whole. This attitude towards reality, which was basic to medieval life, has been maintained by Catholicism, particularly Thomistic Catholicism, and is maintained in modern times by Marxist thought, which, though it denies essence, nonetheless sees reality as one. The French have never accepted the dissociation of body and matter from mind and spirit, suggested by Descartes' philosophy and accepted by Protestantism, which looked upon matter as the source of sin and corruption. Not only has man always been at the centre of French thinking, but the human body has always been looked upon as the basis of man's relationship with the universe, and the senses as necessary and important as the spirit. God is not only the source of the logos; He also uses His hands to lift or to warn man, or to enable Moses or Joshua to perform their miracles,

* De Gaulle's famous remark: *"La réforme oui; la chie-en-lit non!"* confirms this point.

which required physical action. That is why the body and its biological functions are the basis of French thought, art and aphorisms; that is why the French have responded more to a religion like Catholicism, which recognizes the importance of the senses and the importance of the body, than to a religion like Protestantism, which has looked askance at the senses. That is also why they have been so concerned with good living and with the satisfaction of the senses, an attitude which cannot be described as superficial hedonism, while it is, on the contrary, evidence of the importance which the French attach to the idea of the wholeness of man and of an integrated reality.

The English, with their cult of the will, have tended, until recently, to treat the body in a kind of Corneillean fashion, that is to say, as an instrument which, provided it was fit and under full control for action, did not need to be pampered with refined attentions and pleasures. Needless to say, these attitudes have now altered to the point that there is an ostentatious parading of the body, which leaves the matter-of-fact French looking rather overclad and prudish. The French have always called a spade a spade and a nincompoop *un couillon*, unperturbed by any false notion of salaciousness or pudor; they have never hesitated to use straightforward anatomic terminology as a matter of course. The flutter caused in the dovecots of Television House by the use of the English equivalent to the word *foutre* could never have taken place in France, where this word, more than liberally used in everyday conversation, does not bring the faintest of blushes to any cheek.

Another aspect to be noted in connection with the second of the two aphorisms under discussion is that it exhibits the faith in mathematical truth and abstraction which is very much part of the make-up of the French, with whom knowledge has always been knowledge of the essences and objective knowledge, and never, not even with the Positivists, knowledge of particulars, as in England, or subjective Kierkegaardian knowledge. The aphorism which is being discussed could be described as being a mathematical tautology; it implies neither a possibility of moral judgements, nor of development through experience; it is a flat, mathematical impossibility, and its cold logic could only be ignored at the cost of foolishness. The French love for things of the mind and for mathematics is such that, when something is easy to solve and presents to the English mind no trouble or bother, it is summed up by the abstract impersonal statement: *"Il n'y a pas de problème"*. On the other hand, a ticklish situation for an Englishman is nothing of the kind for a Frenchman. It is something serious, fearfully confounding and perhaps downright *terrible*. In short the Frenchman neither overstates nor understates, thereby showing his perfect moral control.

The English, in spite of their respect for the glory of Newton, seem to have preferred, until just recently, character and political leadership to artistic and intellectual achievements, in spite of a unique asset like Shakespeare. They seem to have caught on only recently to the value of artistic prestige. Yet, in the end, it is quite understandable that they should have valued highly, perhaps even above everything else, their political evolution and its achievements, which are certainly unequalled in the world. Once they had got rid of autocratic and tyrannic monarchy, supposedly embodied in Charles I, they managed to evolve, through their liberalism and tolerance, the key elements of their political system, a structure which, in spite of its flaws, has given them centuries of stability and national cohesion. This structure, though it is rather strained now, will, I am sure, survive, until they have again found their equilibrium and their sense of direction. Being much less given than the French to respect the mind and theorizing, they have shown throughout their artistic and political developments a strong sense of organic life, of adaptability and capacity to subsume individualism to the group or to the community, which has enabled them to enjoy well over three centuries of stable political evolution that have led, in the end, to the peaceful creation of a progressive society. Though they are less individualistic than the French, they deeply respect the individual with his quirks and eccentricities, and they generally exhibit tolerance, good humour and a civism, which, I am sure, makes the work of their rulers easier than that of any other country. They have even now, in this rather equalitarian age, an inborn sense of hierarchy as part of the natural order of things, with an aristocracy at the top. The reasons for this are, above all, geographical and historical. Being an island, England has suffered neither invasions nor enemy occupations and has, therefore, enjoyed the kind of stability which has made it possible for her social and political developments to evolve progressively, without too many major crises. This freedom from foreign invasions has saved England, until recently at least, from the excessive administrative and strategic centralization to which France has been compelled by fear of invasion. England, free from such a compulsion, has been able to adopt towards the world at large, and towards Europe in particular, an attitude of wait and see, which no European nation could afford and which, of course, is no longer tenable in our age. English society has never been thrown in its practical entirety into the melting-pot of revolution and fundamental structural changes, as was the case with French society in 1789. Therefore it has not developed like the French a mass consciousness of national social problems and changes.

The English, by and large, do not think in terms of revolution; they think of reforms and evolutions generally envisaged within the context of the existing framework of accepted social and moral values. They will not join in the *Internationale*, and sing *"Du passé faisons table rase"*! They care for their past, and they love their customs and traditions to the point that they form the basis of their legal and constitutional systems. They dislike systems and freshly minted constitutions, which are for them too abstract and too cerebral. They prefer the particular and the concrete and they generally respect the established order. England is not a country of clearcut contrasts and radical changes. The outlines of things are blurred. The social ladder is there all right, but it is not divided into completely separated sections. The English aristocracy, which, unlike the French, had not allowed itself to be discredited or rendered impotent, has adapted itself to changing circumstances and has been throughout the centuries a vital element of English life. It took part in the great commercial and industrial expansion and it contributed greatly to what is called the intelligentsia, which right up to the beginning of the twentieth century was generally part of the dominant class.

French society had, on the contrary, been torn apart by the great Revolution. The French aristocracy had been fully emasculated by Richelieu, and the Monarchs who ruled after him compelled its remainder to live at court, so as to pick up crumbs from the King's table. The outcome of that was that, unlike the English aristocracy, they had, on the whole, no close ties with the people who worked on their lands, nor any sense of duty and responsibility towards them. The result has been that, for a long time, there has been in France a kind of cleavage between rulers and ruled, and that some members of the ruling classes (aristocrats or bourgeois), unable to realize the need for reforms and only concerned with the fulfilment of their acquisitive instincts, have never hesitated, either during the Revolution, in 1870, or in 1940, to collaborate with the enemy, provided that he defended or sought to reestablish the old order. This is something which has not happened and is unlikely to happen in English society, just as it is unlikely that an English general or group of generals would rebel against a government whose political views or solutions they did not approve of. Whatever they may think, they will not rock the boat to such an extent. The French have never hesitated to rock the boat, at any time. They always put principles, personal judgement, and, as in the cases mentioned before, self-interests before civism and duty to the Nation, and that is one of the reasons why France has had such a chequered history of rises and falls. Yet France possesses undying vitality and resilience, and the obscure forces, which are at work and which, beyond the contentiousness of the mind, guide and maintain its forward progress, can always throw forth at the required moment a man of destiny, a Napoleon or a De Gaulle, who inspires them to do great things. The English genius, more organic, more profoundly interwoven with obscure, instinctive forces, cannot be rationalized or analysed; it can only express itself at its best in action, as was the case in 1940 when Churchill refused to surrender, in spite of what looked then like overwhelming odds. In such cases, the English people respond without questioning. The French genius, with its strong rationalistic strain, its uncompromising search for consciousness, individualism and truth, needs to understand itself in order to give its best. When this conviction is achieved either through reason or through passionate faith in ideals, as during the Revolution or during the First World War, then France's energy seems inexhaustible. Contemporary, peaceful France understood a man like De Gaulle who, though he may have had, like any human being, his deaf or blind spots, was able better than any other Frenchman for generations to hear and to detect the true voice and the true gaze of France.

The English respect both the laws and the authority of the

state. The French respect laws, but the state and authority have for long been the objects of an attitude, described by the French as *"Le Système-D"*, which consists in the display of all sorts of skills in order to defeat them or to get, in some small way, the better of them. Where else but in England could one find, at least until recently, so many voluntary organizations? In England, people love to do things without being told. They run, or they used to run, hospitals and social services all on a voluntary basis. In France, from schools to hospitals, it is all state-directed, because the state holds the strings of the purse, therefore, from the *Mairie* to the Department and the Administration in Paris, it gives the orders, and this fits admirably with the French love of order, method and planning.

The love of planning and method, which are the key notions of administration and of the state, are of course strongly counteracted by the individualism of a people, every one of whom thinks that he is as clear-minded as his neighbour and that, come what may, ideas and principles must not be sacrificed. France is the land of ideas, ideals and mottoes—Liberty, Equality, Fraternity, Freedom or Death, etc.—and the result of such devotion to ideas is that the French, thinking themselves all more or less descendants of Descartes, therefore rational, are intolerant and irrational in politics, because they, very often, cannot see the wood for the trees or bend individual pride to make it fit with commonweal. None of the easy two-party system of England, where the two sides can even co-operate and, at times, behave as one. France, as befits a very logical country, must have all political opinions represented; it has therefore a host of parties, which never co-operate; they only strike bargains against a third.

One of the main weaknesses of the French state, in the last few decades, has been a multiplicity of political parties, certainly increased by the system of proportional representation, which has made it practically impossible to establish a government with a solid enough majority to enable it to govern or to carry out any clearcut given programme. In fact, governments were generally coalition governments, and programmes of action were not programmes but improvised sailing charters, so as to enable the government in power to remain afloat as long as possible without running into the various shoals or rocks which beset its course. The

Indo-Chinese and the Algerian wars were the most telling failures of this type of governmental paralysis and reduction of programmes of action to their lowest common denominator of distinctiveness. If one adds to this unsteady foundation of French political life the fact that the various French constitutions, having mostly been conceived in a climate of fear of personal power, had always posited a weak executive, which had practically no means of overruling the power and the inherent fractiousness of the legislative assembly, and, above all, the individualistic and anarchic tendencies of a people who are only united in crises, and who are never closer to explosion than when they seem quiescent and docile, one begins to have an idea of the difficulties of governing them and the kind of political structure required to reconcile their individualism with their love of, and respect for, mental order.

One of the two main weaknesses of the past French constitutions, the weakness of the Executive in relation to the Legislative, has been corrected by the 1958 constitution, which has reasonably increased the power of the President and of the Executive, now strong enough to stand up to the centrifugal forces of the multiplicity of parties and to govern.

The other main weakness, the multiplicity of parties, was certainly attenuated by General de Gaulle's attempt at polarizing French political forces into two groups, a Gaullist and a Communist group, each of them drawing to itself the elements which have something in common with it or which might be moved by the belief that half a loaf is better than no loaf at all. Far from being detrimental to French political life, as some commentators have suggested, the polarization of the existing political parties into two main groups is bound to be beneficial to the Gaullist as well as to the Communist party and, above all, to the country as a whole which will benefit from this piece of Hegelian dialectics, which sharpens thesis and anti-thesis, until one of the two elements absorbs or eliminates the other, or until a final synthesis, which has discarded the extreme aspects of the two contending elements and retains only what can make an organic whole is reached. Incoherent multiplicity, or hydra-like heads, pulling in contrary directions, can only make for paralysis and disintegration. Life and the development of ideas and of social and political structures are dialectical. There is always a polarization towards opposites and a synthesis, with the rejection of extremes, which form thus the nucleus of new polarizations towards new syntheses. A political party with an ideology and a dynamism aimed at fundamental structural changes cannot develop by making common cause with a party which merely shelters behind it, in order to break the walls of the fortress which it would like to occupy, and later to man against all comers, including, of course, its former associates. The Communist party does not need associates. It needs enemies to sharpen its capacity for action and to rally to it those who really believe that it is worth while marching with.

The Gaullist party also needs not half-hearted supporters who say "Yes—but . . .", or who claim to be more radical than it truly is, but enemies who will make it clear that there are only two forms of democracy which are confronting each other. There is Communist democracy, which means a classless, stateless society, something which could only be achieved through intolerance and abolition of individual freedom, through a world-embracing act of Divine Grace, or, something not impossible, through the acceptance of the principle of political democracy by the Communists, and there is politico-economic democracy which, in the future, will seek to abolish society's alienation, while maintaining individual freedom, tolerance and the freely accepted authority of the state as means to implement these objectives. Having won the day, Gaullism will have to be a policy which has understood the revendication of the students and the alienation of the workers, and which therefore has, up to a point, begun to absorb some of the vital elements of the dynamism of the Communist party. The key word, participation, if even given concrete reality in industry, in all aspects of organized social life and in regional and municipal affairs, ought to be the guiding force of a new truly democratic society in France.

The problem for France is to strike a balance between anarchic individualism, on the one side, and love of order, planning and sense of direction, on the other. This balance is difficult to achieve and to maintain, yet it is this balance which must be found; if it is not, France can neither thrive nor play her full part in the community of Nations. It is a balance that must embody a state of equilibrium between the need for order and the need for individual freedom, which, of course, must be carefully watched and constantly adjusted, according to the various changes which occur. This is no easy task, for as De Tocqueville admirably put it: "The French people, indocile by temperament, accommodate themselves better with the arbitrary and even violent authority of a Prince, rather than with the authority of a government freely chosen by its citizens. One day, they are the declared enemy of any form of obedience; another day, they display in obedience the kind of passion that even the nation best gifted for servitude could not achieve. Led with a thread, so long as nobody resists; ungovernable as soon as the example of resistance is given somewhere. Thus they are always deluding their masters, who fear them either too much or too little."*

Fortunate English! They do not need such adjustments to their moral and civic discipline. Their concern being not with thought and ideal but with action and organic life, which can only be maintained if its component parts work together in health and harmony, they find it easy to subsume their love of individual freedom in the harmony of the whole and in the respect for established authority. This authority was, and still is up to a point, finely counterbalanced by regional and corporate authorities of various sorts, though one witnesses now an increasing tendency towards centralization and towards the replacement of voluntarism by legislation. Yet the sense of civism remains such that the party in power is as much concerned with carrying out its programme as with keeping its opponents in a fit state to take over, if and when required. The day when the party in power in France will be genuinely solicitous of the cohesion and moral fibre of the party or parties which oppose it, will certainly be a day for flag-waving and rejoicings.

In England, to rock the boat or not to play the game is no good, whether one is a politician or a cricketer. Anyone who does one or the other cannot be right, and the principles which he may invoke, in order to explain his behaviour, simply cannot hold water. He will be told that what he did was not fair, and that is much more important here than the French notion of *ce n'est pas juste*. Whatever he may say, he will not be right. For the Frenchman, fair or not fair is not very important, if he thinks that reason is on his

* Alexis de Tocqueville, *L'Ancien Régime et la Révolution*.

side. To conform has never been one of the uppermost French traits, at any rate, to conform to a pattern, a convention or an attitude which does not have his intellectual assent. How could he, when since his early age he has been schooled in the notion that what matters is intellectual achievement and not playing in the rugby team or rowing for his university? *Mens sana*, yes, but the *in corpore sano* is something which has been much overlooked until our time, when Anglo-Saxon influence has begun to make itself felt in French education. Times are certainly changing, but until recently the French were not interested in school sports, and they set a much higher premium on mental gymnastics than on pure and simple gymnastics. The English mistrust the intellect; the word 'clever' has a distinctly pejorative meaning, and they are too concerned with the concrete, too pragmatic to indulge in mental acrobatics and in systems and set rules. What matters is doing, and that means that one can only know exactly what ought to be done once the action which engages the will and the attention has been performed. So the rule in England is don't cross your bridges before you come to them, everything in its own good time, and there is a time for everything, something which the mind cannot disturb, because reality and matter are not abstractions, but things to be dealt with through time and the senses.

A great deal of the misunderstanding between the French and the English is due to the innate empiricism and utilitarianism of the latter and the rationalizing and theorizing leanings of the former. Where the Frenchman maintains that something cannot be done, until he has grasped its mental structure and unfolding, the Englishman says we should go ahead and see what is required once action has started. This is a gap which must, and can be, bridged, but it is certainly no use describing the Frenchman as obstinate because he wishes to grasp the pattern of a thing before he undertakes to perform it, and it is also no use to describe the Englishman as unco-operative because he believes that action is a way of thinking, and thinking is a way of not acting. Descartes may have said, "I think, therefore I am", but he did not say, "I think, therefore I do", and that is what matters for the Englishman, who truly *is* when he is doing something. He does not even say: "I think we should do this or that", but "I *feel* we should do this or that"; his thinking is more biological and generalized and, in this respect, is more feminine than the cerebral French. And the feminine element, strange as it may seem in connection with "this happy breed of men", who claim to be, and are, virile, is not without foundation. The English are virile for action, but they are, in spite of their well-schooled, well-tempered self-control, more deeply emotional than the French, or, should I say, to be precise, more capable of purely emotional reactions, because their emotions, though controlled, are not, as is generally the case with the French, processed by mind. The result is that there is in England more sentimentality, which is, above all, emotion unprocessed by mind, than there is in France. The French, at least some of them, are less self-controlled in gesture and in behaviour, because they do not believe in the need for such self-control. They believe, on the contrary, in doing openly what they want to do, and they believe that morality is more a matter of individual conscience than of group or society judgement. Nevertheless, both Flaubert and Baudelaire had ground to realize that this was not quite so. Yet, on the whole, it is more so than in England. The French are mentally passionate. Pascal only believed in ideas for which men were prepared to die, and Stendhal's heroes are more intent on conquest than on true passion. Those of Laclos belong to the same school. The Englishman controls his emotions or his feelings as he controls a pack of horses; the Frenchman has his emotions so well processed by mind that, on the whole, they do not attempt to challenge its authority. Two brief remarks are here necessary. The first is to the effect that the corrective "on the whole" is the operative part of the sentence, for if its validity were to be tested in Marseilles, Nice or Toulon, where the Italian element is strong, it would be found wanting. The second is that pride, which is a complex of intellect and feeling, and which is the natural concomitant of the strong individualism of the French, can cause emotional and irrational outbursts of greater violence than emotions or feelings. *"Je suis maître de moi comme de l'univers"*, said Sévère in *Polyeucte*, and he was the perfect gentleman, *l'honnête homme* of his time, the living reproach to those Racinian characters who were swept away by their atavistic, inborn passions, as if Descartes had never existed. Of course, what matters for the Racinian characters is that, however swept away by their passions they may be, they have at the same time a heart-rending lucidity about what they are doing, what happens to them and what they are. They live and die under the glare of the most ruthless analysis, which, by the time it is completed, makes it clear that death and darkness are the only unavoidable means of putting an end to this merciless light. Indeed, it is this power of analysis which, from Montaigne to Pascal, Racine, Vauvenargues, La Rochefoucauld, Maine de Biran, Sartre and Camus, all descendants of St. Augustine, is characteristic of the French mind, which, at times, goes so far in this direction as to be thoroughly paralysed and inhibited about action. France is in fact a country of moralists where people's morality seems to be, on the whole, hedonistic, that is to say, they are neither sadists nor masochists; they believe in the pleasures of the senses and of good living, but certainly not in immorality. Strong family ties, a very much alive religious faith, and the fact that the majority of France's population live in smallish or medium size agglomerations, combine to produce a reasonably strict morality. England has produced not moralists but moral art, and it respects morality to the point of intolerance, while it is, and has been, the land of political tolerance for generations. Where would Voltaire, St. Evremond, Chateaubriand have gone without England? On the other hand, what could Oscar Wilde have been without England?

Until the last war, the English were self-confident, without undue need for self-assertion or competitiveness. They were, in fact, glad to describe themselves, in many ways, as amateurs, not professionals. Now things have changed. We are living in a world of growing professionalism and ever expanding technology. This country has had, willy-nilly, to come to grips with these problems, and the transition has not been easy, for it cannot be easy to pass from a rock-like sense of security and rigid morality to uncertainty of status and relativity of values. The result has been hesitancy, on the one side, and a real explosion of exuberance, on the other. The young have really flung their bonnets over the windmills, and they have shown that, even if the economy is sluggish, they are not. They are full of life and ideas, unorthodox though some may be, and certainly remote enough from those of their Victorian grandparents.

At this moment, having found herself suddenly trimmed on the sides, shorn of a vast domain which was the Empire, and outstripped in power by the U.S.A., Russia, and, very soon, by rising China, this country, suffering from a lack of sense of direction and place, has tried to replace the idea of Empire with the idea of Commonwealth. The substitution offers only an appearance of strength, without the reality of power and without any possibility of real unity of purpose in the social, economic and doctrinal fields. The Atlantic Alliance, with its special relationship with the U.S.A., is also a substitute for lost power and a means to keep up illusions, and it is because of these two illusions, probably more than anything else, that Britain first averted her eyes from Europe, then reluctantly changed her mind, without wholehearted conviction and recently sought participation in a manner which her friends, who have faith in her and want her as part of Europe, would have preferred to have been different. That is to say, it should have been more of a quiet approach, based on a profound desire to create a new Europe,* and less like some kind of para-military operation aimed at achieving a spectacular success which would impress both participants and onlookers. The underlying weaknesses of this attitude are made clear by the fact that this country seems to be practically as much in the throes of autocriticism as France in the nineteen thirties. That an intellectual nation like France should, under the impact of the failure of ideals, turn into a combination of a M. Teste watching his mind at work and a Gidean character scrutinizing his conscience is understandable. But that England should do so can only be explained by the awareness of both the failure and the impossibility of action, in a world in which action now only pertains to the two biggest powers on earth and could in fact very well lead to disaster. So England's young generation has partly adopted the attitude of the French towards the Establishment and institutions, until recently beyond criticism, satire or laughter. The political parties have lost their clearcut differences, and they no longer reflect the full spectrum of political attitudes and beliefs. The disillusionment towards politicians has not gone as far as it had gone in France between the wars and after, but it is nevertheless present and fully confirmed by the fear that the failures of the party in power

* This seems to me to be the case now, and everyone who cares for the creation of a new Europe hopes that this country will soon be part of it as she is part of its civilization.

37

might not be automatically made good by its opponent. Thence a certain feeling of frustration, the outcome of which is, for the moment, nothing more than a touch of voluntarism with the Back Britain campaign, some student unrest or a suggestion that technicians should play a greater part than they do in government.

The adaptability, the robust common sense and democratic traditions of this country will surmount these passing difficulties, reform what needs to be reformed, and rediscover its historic sense of direction and place in the world, for the world would not be what it is without it, and, as a Frenchman, I feel that no country is more immeshed and interested than France in the life of this country. I should also like to say two things which seem to me important. The first is that, whoever the successors of De Gaulle may be, his contribution to France's stability and prestige and to the New Europe will be recognized. Instead of a country half-stifled in the tentacles of factions and colonial wars as France was when De Gaulle came to power, we have now a country which has succeeded in transforming a previously strife-laden colonial relationship into an adult partnership between equals. Instead of a country ever in the throes of chronic financial and political crises, we have a country which has enjoyed ten years' stability in both of these fields. De Gaulle certainly understood the inherent weaknesses of the French political ethos and he tried to attend to it through the establishment of a semi-presidential régime which provided stability without infringement to freedom. But, of course, political institutions are only what men make of them, and it remains to be seen what the French will do without De Gaulle.

Secondly, De Gaulle made of France a much more solid and reliable friend of this country than his opponents would have done, because he had ideas and principles which he was not prepared to barter for anything. He happened to believe that Europe could best contribute to the peace of the world and to the equilibrium of civilization by being able to make its own voice heard amid the voices of the U.S.A. and Russia. This does not imply any kind of enmity or prejudices; on the contrary, it implies both pragmatism and idealism. Pragmatism makes it clear in more than one way that a country partly committed to the kind of ideology to which the U.S.A. has been officially committed, until now, can only be accepted, not as a dominant partner, but as a partner from whom one must, at times, without animosity, but on the contrary with regret, dissent. In order to be able to do that, Europe must be a country of truly equal partners, and not a pyramidal structure like the out-dated Atlantic Alliance in which wisdom is measured in terms of military strength or economic power. If it were so, the influence of this country or of France on shaping the world would be very small indeed. So would have been the impact of Greece as compared with that of the empire of Darius; yet history has proved that it was the other way round. The world and civilization can survive only through ideals, whether Christian or Buddhist, of which the most important is "Thou shalt not kill", and the best "Thou shalt love thy neighbour as thyself". That does not mean disdainful or pious love from a distance, but concrete, beneficent love which insists upon the sharing of the joys and the well-being, as well as the sorrows, of the Earth. In an age of gratuitous, purely destructive violence, nothing is more important than the sixth commandment. If de-creation or destruction is part of creation, if any transformation requires breaking up of component parts, rejection, and, on the human plane, suffering, they are only so as part of a pattern and fluidity which aims at increasing and enriching life. On the human and historical plane, violence necessarily breeds violence, and society must either evolve peacefully or bleed itself to death through strife and anarchy. The massive spread of education and information, the creation of a kind of world-wide consciousness, the vast improvement in all aspects of life, are calling forth a new age in which the old political and social structures which divided human society into governors and governed, leaders and followers, will be replaced by a vast complex of democratic institutions which, applied at all levels of social life, such as the church, the universities, the factories, the commercial enterprises, the various regions which compose a country, will enable the individual to take an active part in the decision-making, which before was the privilege of the central authority, whatever it was.

The May madness, fiesta, or happening which took place in France in 1968 is symptomatic of the anxiety and dissatisfaction which afflicts, in varying degrees, the technological societies of the world. It is an image of the disequilibrium of these societies seen through the prism of a country which has long democratic and revolutionary traditions. It is, therefore, something which ought to be taken as a serious sign of the importance of the latent strength of the forces in conflict, and of the urgency of a search for an equilibrium corresponding to the aspirations of a world in the throes of swift and profound change. The main problem which confronts technological society is the problem of individual freedom in a world of computers, monopolies, mass production, conformism and skilfully or autocratically enforced mechanical uniformity. Whether in the democracies or in the totalitarian states there is a more or less wide gap between governing techno-crats and the governed masses, who are becoming more and more aware that they have too little, or even no, say in the shaping of their lives and destiny. The totalitarian states endeavour to maintain alive a climate of fervour and apocalytism in which every one is supposed to work for the good of the régime, which is always threatened by foreign subversion and latent or open aggression. Heaven, or a kind of paradisical state, lies at the end of the communist journey, which, however, hard, is worth mak-ing. Besides, there is not much chance of swerving right or left, for authority, solidly based on the party technocrats and military power, ruthlessly crushes any attempt at non-conformity. The synthesis of Marxist dialectics is not the abolition of the state and the emergence of a freely creative society, but the emergence of an autocratic state intent on maintaining the régime by force and repression. Still, in spite of the strength of authority, whether in Czechoslovakia, Poland, Eastern Germany or Spain, young people have shown that they are dissatisfied with the state of things and that they want something different. They do not quite know what, but they want above all to be able, if not to transform things, at least to destroy what is, and to exercise their opposition to the ruling values and the established order.

The revolutions of the past were upsurges of oppressed peoples, whether peasants or workers, against their masters and demands for better conditions of life. These upsurges, the philosophy of which is best represented by various forms of socialism and Marxism, are playing no part in the present revolt and wide-spread anarchy against the various established orders. Marxism, applied or theoretical, is irreconcilable with anarchy or with the notion of permanent revolt. It is in fact too rationalistic, too concerned with economic conditions and also too firmly eschatological, to be reduced to an attitude of romantic revolt and gratuitous action. The working class is aware of itself as a class, and the men who compose it are too conscious of their responsibilities as members of a group, of a class and of the future, to indulge in action for action's sake. That is why the workers and the communist or socialist parties which embody their aspirations are unlikely to make common cause with the students' protests.

The western world has now had a quarter of a century without any major war, and the wars which have taken place, whether in Algeria, Vietnam or Biafra, have profoundly divided public opinion and, on the whole, have alienated youth from authority in all its forms. In the U.S.A., the war in Vietnam has torn the nation apart; in Europe, it has given a battle-cry and a banner to the opposition against authority and the older generations. Everywhere, it is a catalyst drawing to it the forces of discontent against those who have and those who order other people's lives in a world overplanned and, for many, shorn of hope in the future. The machinery of protest was therefore ready and well trained, and when concern with the war in Vietnam diminished, it quickly turned and exploded in other directions. France seemed prosperous and at peace, and yet, without warning, a few groups of students could unleash a movement which soon involved the whole country and, for a brief moment, threatened the state. But contrary to 1789 or 1848 it was not a revolution, it was a revolt, a conflagration of contending notions mostly verbal, confined to a few Oedipal funereal pyres, represented by the burning of cars, and the occupation of two ancestral homes—the Sorbonne and the Odéon. All that, aided and stimulated by television, radio, press and onlookers, culminated in a display of total theatre, played in the streets of Paris and of the various main cities of France, with millions of actors and spectators, all enjoying their respective performances. This was typically French, and Sartre, putting on his philosophic bonnet, gravely described it as a love of praxis, something which connects this kind of nihilistic, histrionic ebullience with Marxism and Existentialism. It is a fact that when one has children, brain children, one is reluctant to see them die. Sartre does his best to save his. Hats off to him who seems to believe that St. Vitus's dance is superior to any *cogito* or to any notion of "Look before you leap". "Leap and keep on leaping" seems to have been the motto of these kinetic performers of May Day in Paris; "if you don't leap, talk about it and run down the bourgeois—in the majority of cases, your father". One had there the making of what the Scots call a fine clamjanfrie, and the southern part of France and Spain, a *fiesta*, with young animals let loose through a town, to the merriment of the population. All would have been well without the workers and the political parties, who felt that their clothes were being stolen right from their backs; so, half naked, and unprepared, they leapt into the breach, trying to snatch some of the spoils, and some of them went as far as to trade the government's skin, before the animal was well and truly dead. They forgot De Gaulle, who had more than one life and who, in no time, was back in the fray, and, with the support of the army and the bulk of the French people, sent the reckless revellers back to plain living and porridge, and to a reckoning as to who would pay for the broken crockery and other things.

The cost was quite high for France, and the results could be disastrous if the profound and grave causes of this brief effervescence were ignored. The main cause is the lack of individual freedom and responsibility in societies which, on the one hand, because of the breakdown of religious and social morality, advocate individual morality, and on the other, because of the highly mechanical structure of these societies devoted to technology, high production and consumption, through all sorts of pressures, make it impossible for the individual to feel anything but a drop of water in a stream which rolls him forwards. The moment a member of a technological society takes up a job or a profession, he becomes hedged in by various responsibilities, controls, form filling, artificial needs and demands so that, though he regularly casts his vote when asked to do so, he feels he has no great hold on his destiny, run as it is by highly centralized bureaucratic machinery. This is true for France, and for the Continent, and the U.S.A. even, more than it is true for Britain.

Young people, who have not yet been fully harnessed into, or corsetted, by responsibilities, feel all the more the weight of these restrictions and the hopelessness of the future; they are, on the whole, deprived of sufficient means of making their influence felt. As ideals are at a low ebb, as the rat-race is becoming fiercer and fiercer and the world of imagination has been more and more shrunk by discoveries and explorations, they naturally seek to redress, most of them in a reasonable way, the wrongs which deprive them of hope and individual freedom. The age of respect for authority, whatever it is, is past. Fathers, and God the Father Himself, are either rejected or contested, and with a world-wide system of information, and constant stimulation, young people, critically-minded and aware of their strength and of their vast contribution to the consumer society, want to have a greater say in its running, and a few of them, intoxicated by nihilism, want to destroy it. In France, the alternative to destruction of the state was either the Communist party or the army, and the bulk of the French people made it clear that it wanted neither. So, one can only hope that the bourgeois having had their cold shower and the sons of these same bourgeois having let off steam and made their views and their needs clear, the state will seriously endeavour to redress the balance between the satisfied adults and the dissatisfied, distressed young people, without forgetting the urgent need to improve the fate of the workers, manual and others, whose earnings are insufficient. In order to achieve this, the young and the workers will have to go on pressing for reforms from what is called the establishment—the rulers, the haves or what one likes. But these have great resilience and elasticity; they know how to flatter, to deflate would-be rebels by inebriating them with publicity, attention and gadgets of all kinds, which blunt the edge of dissatisfaction and the longing for freedom, and slowly turn them into ladder-climbers and good candidates for their fathers' places.

III

Cultures

What are the respective cultures of Britain and France? Without attempting any detailed histories of the life and arts of the two countries, a prospect which is well beyond the scope of this brief essay, we shall first try to see what could be meant by the word culture, and how far one can differentiate it from the word civilization. Before attempting this disquisition, one ought, I think, if not to enumerate laboriously, at least to hint at some of the reasons why art may be used as the principal means through which one can try to distinguish between British and French culture. Here are some of these reasons. Although we may think, and we generally do, that a given style, a certain aspect of art, expresses a given society, the true fact is that we only know and see this given society through its art and its actions. So, although it is true to say that, as the appearance and the various phenomenal aspects of society express the true being or noumenon of that society, it is also true that we can only know the noumenon through the phenomenon. One must also bear in mind the fact that art expresses not only a given society at a given time, but, since it is the being of this given society, it is continuous, and so it links past and present to the future, that is to say, to the various aspects of this society and other related societies, which, together, form a whole civilization. If art is valuable and significant in the sense that it truly expresses real important values, its vitality is continuous; if it is insignificant, purely ephemeral and a matter of fashion, it is automatically cast into the shadows and forgotten by what comes after. Its value is always determined by its lastingness and by the creative importance which it maintains within the pattern to which it belongs, and which is constantly altered and revalued by the new creations which are added to it. Art, no less than man, is not an isolated

44

gesture or point in an imaginary vacuum. Man is not man in isolation; man is by essence more than one, and, as such, he is part of a whole—society, history, and creation. Art is not only individual expression, but also the expression of a given society and of history which are shaped by the traditions and the values which art has already established and will continue to establish until the end of the civilization to which it belongs. The supreme works of art, the works of true genius, always face up to, and resolve, the conflict of good and evil, and re-establish the equilibrium and justice which is the essence of life seen *sub specie aeternitatis*. They always both sum up and dominate their time, which they transcend. The second-rate works, the works of talent or very minor genius, cannot reach this state of equilibrium and justice which implies absolute morality, that is to say, the morality of divine or transcendental resolutions; they are therefore lopsided, self-conscious expressions of aspects of the sensibility of their age. They do not, like the works of true genius, naturally rise in harmony over their age; they, on the contrary, remain embedded in it as sectional samples of protest against it or of wilful attempts at harmonizing with what seems to be the tone and fashion of their age.

Can one equate culture with civilization? It seems just as hazardous to do so as it is difficult to discriminate accurately and convincingly between the one and the other. To begin with, it seems evident that the word civilization is obviously more wide ranging than the word culture. One talks, for instance, of "western civilization", but one rarely talks, at least so it seems, of western culture. In a similar way, one talks of Egyptian, Sumerian, Greek or Roman civilizations, but in such cases one would not, on the whole, use the word culture as an equivalent or an alternative to the word civilization. It seems to me that the word civilization has a wider meaning than the word culture and that a given civilization can be made to embrace or to contain many cultures, while one cannot reasonably talk of any given culture embracing many civilizations.

It seems to me that the basic difference between the range and meaning of the two terms is due to the fact that a civilization necessarily implies a religion, transcendental or even nominally materialistic like Marxism, for it seems clear that there is no civilization which did not, and does not, carry with it a religious attitude, or an attitude which, although it might claim to be purely materialistic, implies nevertheless a sense of transcendence, that is to say, an *ideal* concept of man which it aims at perpetuating and enriching. In fact, a civilization is important in relation to the concept of man that it reveals and to the values which this concept carries with it. A concept of man which is totally shorn of any religious or transcendental notions could only foster and bring forth a form of life ruled by sensualism, arbitrariness and force, therefore a form of life condemned, in the end, to self destruction.

Materialism, leaving aside its distant and superficial Greek roots, is a philosophical doctrine which has been evolved within the context of western civilization, and mostly by English and French thinkers. Medieval nominalism is one of its component elements, and its real founder is Francis Bacon, according to whom the senses are infallible and the source of all knowledge. The most important quality of matter is motion, and motion is either caused, or self-caused. If it is caused, one falls straight into metaphysics and into notions of transcendence and finality; if it is self-caused, that is to say, animated with individualizing and complexifying forces of being, then, one still falls into metaphysics, for these forces which are self-caused must necessarily carry with them the finality which animates their causation. There is no hazard in life, and what looks like spontaneous mutations of cells, soon, through what looks like trials and errors, finds its place in the individuating and complexifying growth of life towards self knowledge. Marx repudiated idealism, yet he talked about human nature and about the Eternal. "What is the kernel of evil?" he asked, and the reply was, according to him, "that the individual locks himself in his empirical nature against his eternal nature". Buddhism, which denies, in principle, the divine origin of Buddha, is nevertheless a transcendental faith, the aim of which is to shed matter and to escape forever from the wheel of life. This aim connects the Hegelian dream of spiritualizing matter with the Platonic notion of the real as the absolute and Eternal, which is also non-Being or the Nirvana of Buddhism. Before Plato or Buddha, Pythagoras had said: "We are strangers in the world, and the body is the tomb of the soul, and yet we

46

must not seek to escape by self-murder, for we are the chattels of God, who is our herdsman, and without His command we have no right to make our escape. In this life, there are three kinds of men, just as there are three sorts of people who come to the Olympic Games. The lowest class is made up of those who come to buy and sell, the next above them are those who compete. Best of all, however, are those who come simply to look. The greatest purification of all is, therefore, disinterested science, and it is the man who devotes himself to that, the true philosopher, who has most effectually released himself from the wheel of birth." Chinese civilization is also, like Buddhism, based, in principle, upon a non-transcendental type of faith or set rules of behaviour; yet the Son of Heaven and the Heaven which it posits are transcendental notions. From the simplest fetishism of Central African or Australian tribes, to the worship of the dead and the salvation of the soul in Egypt and in Greece, or the worship of the Sun of Mayan civilization, there is, in all these civilizations, an element of transcendence, a sense of going beyond the finite, the human and matter, which is the true basis of any religious attitude.

While, therefore, one cannot posit a civilization without some form of religion or of religious feeling, it seems to me that one could, on the contrary, talk of aspects of a given culture, without necessarily implying a religion to hold it together and to give it a spiritual sense of continuity and growth. Yet, of course, a culture being always part of a civilization, either as a subdivision or as an aspect of it, carries with it, if it is viewed as part of the whole to which it belongs, the notion of religion. Although the word culture has many meanings, the primary meaning of culture seems to be that of a way of life, and a way of life which can apply to one individual only, as well as to a group, a region, a class, a society, or a whole nation. Yet, on the whole, the word culture is not made coeval with the word civilization. We talk of Scottish, Welsh, French or English cultures, we talk of provincial, rural or urban cultures, but we could hardly talk of western culture in the all-embracing terms in which we talk of western civilization. Besides that, the word culture is often equated with education and learning or with varying degrees of proficiency in a given skill, to say nothing of the well known notions of low-brow and high-brow cultures. The only brief comment to be made in this connection seems to be that it would be utterly unwarranted to equate culture with learning, for culture implies balance, equilibrium of forces between feelings and intellect and between morality and appetites, so as to form a whole or a synthesis which can play a constructive part in the society or the group to which it necessarily belongs. If one accepts the view that such notions are basic to culture, then it ought to be evident that an illiterate person, wise, humane and rationally cooperative with his fellow beings, is more cultured than a highly proficient performer whose only mastery is that of his own skill, and whose only aim is his own self-interest, for if such were the canons by which every individual lived, there could not be any culture; there could only be anarchy and jungle law.

What does one mean by a national culture, in what way could one talk of French culture or of British culture? It seems to me that the attempt to define what one means by a national culture, can be and is generally equated with that of trying to define what one means by what is described as the genius of a given nation, that is to say, by trying to ascertain what differentiates the ethos and the spiritual life of a given nation from that of other nations. Here it must be noted that attempts at establishing clearcut spiritual demarcation lines between nations, and particularly between nations which belong to the same civilization, and which therefore have a great deal in common, are fraught with all sorts of dangers, and can only, in fact, produce either dogmatic generalizations or, purely and simply, tentative and partial truths.

IV

Common Heritage

France and Britain have so much in common, as nations, that the similarities are much more important than the differences. They have similar ethnical origins, the same religion, even the same monarchy to begin with, and, either through peace or war, there exists between them such an uninterrupted continuity of inter-changes that there is not one moment of the history of the world, for the last 2,000 years, when these two peoples were not exchanging ideas, customs, blows, compliments or complaints. As people, we are members of the same family and we have spent a good deal of time wrangling, arguing, pinching each other's property, but also exchanging ideas and mutual respect, and to-gether we have made quite a reasonable contribution to the building of western civilization. Above all, we have drunk at the same sources, admired and followed the same lights, and we have developed the same aspirations and the same dreams. Though our respective feelings may lie deep under our skins, yet even these are very similar, in spite of the colour of the skins or the climates in which men live. But even more important than the basic similarity of feeling is the fact that our thoughts, and I mean the thoughts of Britain and France and of Western Europe in general, spring, first and foremost, from the quays of the Aegean sea which weaves to and fro by the shores of the Piraeus and the walls of the Acropolis. The first names which made human brains immortal are Greek names; they are those of Homer, Aeschylus, Sophocles, Heraclitus, Anaximander, Py-thagoras, Plato, Aristotle, and Socrates. We have learnt practic-ally everything we know from them, and whether we try, like Einstein, to discover the identity of the laws of the universe by mathematical equations, or proclaim with A. N. Whitehead that the whole of western philosophy is only a series of footnotes to Plato, it is to the Athens of these extraordinary geniuses that we owe one of the two greatest revelations or upsurges of light that the world has ever known. They not only planted in man the seeds of the respect for God's most precious gifts to man, which are reason and rationality, they also taught us how to feel and how to discover in the dark caves of the human soul the cobweb-like structures which form the human psyche. The great tragedians, whose words enthralled the crowds that listened to them at the foot of the Parthenon, showed us, before any attempts at scientific explorations of the subconscious or of dreams, the very texture of the unchanging human soul, and both the triumph of man through reason over fate and the triumph of genius through art over man's destiny. Socrates, as deeply inspired by divine wisdom as any man has ever been, told men to look into the mirror which each carries in himself, that is to say, his soul, and to try to descry in it the double which it reflects, for this double is both his true self and also a reflection of the divinity which has entwined itself with it and which will, in the end, reabsorb it into its wholeness. It is the "know thyself" of Socrates which is part both of the enquiring and the humanizing spirit of the west, and also of western man's respect for the inner self which is a reflection of the Divine, and which, as such, must be attended to and treated as something sacred, for this self, washed and sifted by the waters of time, is finally reduced to the pure diamond which forms its core and which Eternity will recognize and welcome back into its perfection. This Eternity, whether as the goal of the Eleusinian mysteries, or as the notion of the great "One" which, according to Plato and Plotinus, looks upon the phenomenal world as a reflection of the idea, and upon knowledge as an illuminating insight into the relationship between these two worlds, blends with immanentist, Judaic Eternity, to produce the time and history-made Eternity of the Christian faith.

The blend of these two strands, the Hellenic and the Judaic, forms the basis of the individual, Christian humanism, and of the sense of the importance of man in creation which pertains not only to Britain and France, but to the whole of western civilization. This basic truth of western civilization had already been summed up in the words which Protagoras uttered two thousand five hundred years ago, "man is the measure of all things", and of course it is not man as an end in himself, idolator of his own power, and the prey of his own desires, ambitions and instincts, but man ruled by reason, symbolized by Athene—the most sacred daughter of the Gods. This was the reason which advocated moderation in all things and which was so respected by Gods and men that it could reconcile not only man and man but also man and the Gods, when the latter had tricked the former into disobeying them for their sport and for their own all too human failings.

Faith in reason and all that it entails, and faith in reality, as part of the rational and the Eternal world, have been the twin lights which have guided western civilization towards finding ways of constantly, though at times painfully slowly, improving the human condition and of increasing its control upon itself as well as upon the natural world, of which it is part. If one were to relate these views to a theology which expresses them at their best and has played a vital part in fostering them, it is to that of Thomas of Aquinas that they should be related. Whatever Thomism is, it certainly is a realistic philosophy, in the sense that, according to it, the apprehension of the real is not a mental construction, but something which exists in its own right, through God's subsistent essence to which it is related, and in the light of which it is judged. In this philosophy, the transcendent is also immanent, and it is through the knowledge of immanence that man can rise to the supra-rational knowledge of transcendence. Augustinianism, which forms the other panel of the Christian dyptich, is closely related to the Hellenic aspects of Christianity represented by Platonism and neo-Platonism. It looks upon transcendence not so much as a subsistent cause of reality but rather as the final goal and aspiration of this reality. Through meditation or mystical experience, reality can merge with transcendence, and in fact, it can only know itself or know what it is, by merging with transcendence through the logos. Thomism itself is deeply grounded in Greek roots, for, if its existential aspect and sense of history implying a present, a past and a future, determined by the present, are Judaic, its rationalist respect for reality, and for the need to humanize it, are Greek. Socrates advocated the knowledge of self in order to do away with ignorance and "to tend his soul". Know-

51

ledge was, for him and for Plato, a voyage of discovery towards the true reality, and the way by which one could pass from a state of ignorance to that of knowledge required not only reason but also moments of unexplainable illumination, which foreshadowed Augustinian Grace and Pascalian and Kierkegaardian revelation. For Plato as well as for Augustine, one can only be saved through divine predestination, that is to say, through divine grace. The true wisdom of Plato, the fount of western mysticism, is nothing else but the orientation of the soul towards grace, and a reconciliation, through meditation, between Life's sorrows and shortcomings and Godly perfection and bliss. The more one knows, the more one is free from all the weaknesses of human nature; therefore, knowledge is freedom, and of course this equating of knowledge with freedom rejoins Hegel. On the other hand, the search for union or perfect harmony with the "One" or with God, through meditation, moments of Grace or transcendence of the contingent, is another aspect of perfect freedom which brings together Platonism and Christianity. As we know Socrates' teaching only through Plato, we therefore have in Plato the two main aspects of human knowledge, and his philosophy embraces not only the Western world but also a good deal of the thought of the East, whose ideal Not-Being rejoins the *One* of Plato, which is both Being and Not-Being. This is not surprising, since Greek philosophy was permeated with Syriac, Egyptian and Iranian philosophy. Besides that, the fact that many of the great fathers of the church were of Middle-Eastern origin, and the contribution of the great Muslim philosophers, increased this influence.

These fundamental beliefs, which determine the attitude that one has towards life, and, something which is more important still, towards death, underlie western civilization and make it easy to understand why, throughout the centuries, there has been such an interpenetration of feelings and thoughts between western nations and particularly between Britain and France, whose developments in all fields of human endeavour and, above all, in the arts, in science and in the political and social fields are complementary and at times indistinguishable one from the other. Right from the collapse of the Roman Empire, throughout the periods described respectively as the Dark Ages and the Middle Ages, up to the end of the Hundred Years War, long periods during which all men of the western world were united in their creatureliness and were unaffected by any restrictive parochialism, the comings and goings between the aristocracies, the various religious orders, and what could be called the intellectuals of the two countries, were such as to make it difficult to talk of specifically English or French cultures. Life in both countries was so similar as to be undifferentiated, and in the fields of ideas and of the arts the differences were practically non-existent. The Channel then was not a barrier but a link. The Celts, our common ancestors, had come and gone between Gaul and Albion, and their imagination, their sense of mystery which connects them with the Greeks, had not been fully obliterated by Roman military might and love of order. The religious orders which flourished in the so-called Dark Ages continued to show that England and France were one single country. Norman art and Gothic art span the two countries. There is hardly a religious centre in France which does not have a connection with England. What a surprise, for instance, to arrive in a small town of Berry, called Saint Menoux, and to discover that it and the remarkable Norman church which is its chief ornament owe their name to an Irish monk, Menoux, of the eighth century. Menoux, Bishop of Quimper, went to Rome on a pilgrimage and, on his return, he stopped at St. Menoux, where he died. He had asked to be buried there. His remains are said to have miraculous effects on people afflicted with nervous troubles or disorders. The sufferer has simply to place his head in a hole, in the little stone coffin behind the altar, which contains some relics of the Saint, and pray for a cure; the holy relics do the rest. Such is the power of holy Irish bones buried in French soil!

The Venerable Bede, great founder of monasteries, and his pupil St. Boniface, who became Pope, made of England a centre of learning, and when Charlemagne wanted to establish a new system of education in his vast domain, he asked Alcuin, born in York, and a disciple of Bede, to cross the Channel and found the famous *École du Palais*, which paved the way for the University of Paris and for the development of rational knowledge. Alcuin was succeeded in 847 by John the Scot or Erigina, Irish-born thinker, who is the most original mind of the ninth century. Pelagian, Platonist and pantheist, he held daring views which were condemned by the church but which he could defy, thanks to the sustained patronage of Charles the Bold. His great work, *De Divisione Naturae*, gives a full interpretation of the Universe and sets, for the first time in Christianity, philosophy on the same plane as theology. Revelation and reason both being sources of truth, they cannot, according to him, come into conflict, and, if and where they seem to do so, reason is to be preferred, "for authority comes from reason, and any authority not founded on true reason is lacking in strength". These, at the time when they were pronounced, were bold words which were the basis of rationalist thinking, and of a form of rationalism which developed and maintained a flavour of its own more Platonist than Aristotelian.

Plato and Aristotle, Augustine and Aquinas, these were the two poles between which western thought oscillated. But perhaps instead of talking of poles, something which implies equality of strength of attraction and importance, it might be better to talk of the dialectics of the development of thought, in the sense that the basis, or the thesis, of western thought is Plato, criticized or modified by Aristotle, working towards a form of synthesis which is finally achieved with Hegel.

In the Middle Ages, the Church, the greatest authority of the western world, is truly international; it knows no national frontiers, and Kings and Emperors acknowledge its authority. The lesson taught to Henry IV of Germany who was made to pace about, barefoot, in the snow of Canossa, waiting for a forgiving nod from Pope Gregory VII, sank in, and its import lasted for nearly four centuries. Whatever its weaknesses, the Catholic Church was truly catholic. Bishops and Cardinals were appointed anywhere in western Europe, irrespective of their places of birth, and they went as teachers to the great centres of learning. English-born John of Salisbury was Bishop of Chartres, and one of its foremost teachers, where he continued the Platonist traditions and the humanism of his famed predecessor, John the Scot. The noble Cathedral of Chartres had just been completed in 1164, and John of Salisbury's great contemporaries were the Abbot of Cluny, Peter Abélard, the great Anselm, Italian-born Archbishop of Canterbury, and Suger, Abbot of St. Denis. Anselm and Abélard are again two aspects of the dyptich or of the dialectic of Christianity. Anselm's words, "I must believe, so that I may understand", are answered by

Abélard's, "I must understand so that I may believe". Before Anselm, another Archbishop of Canterbury, Augustine, had shared his views; after him, up to a point, Pascal, and later, in full agreement with him, Kierkegaard, approached faith in the same way.

Beyond Abélard, master of rationalism, we can see Aquinas, and later still, Descartes, Montesquieu and all those who pursue truth through the questionings and questings of the mind. The Abbé Suger was not so much on the side of Aristotle and the rationalists as against the belief that abstraction and the pursuit of pure ideas could be within everybody's mental capabilities. He, on the contrary, believed that "the average mind can only rise to truth through what is material". This is not only an assertion of the importance of matter but, above all, of the belief that religious truth has to be mediated by symbols, representations and artistic objects. The way to God is therefore through the beautiful creations of man. This attitude to art is perfectly consonant with a society which was beginning to feel the first touches of well-being and prosperity and was evolving a new ethos, an ethos which allowed an important place to the refinements of living and to feeling, and a greater and greater importance to the feminine element in life and therefore to women. It was the age of Eleanor of Aquitaine, of the troubadours, courtly love and courtly romances, an age in which woman, sung, praised and worshipped as never before or since, occupied a very high place in society. In religion this corresponds to the growing cult of the Holy Virgin, the great mediator, which becomes the most important aspect of Catholicism and of religious art. Human and divine love opened new vistas to men, and just at that time, the most lovable saint of Christendom, St. Francis, was born at Assisi in Tuscany. He founded the Franciscan order, which has played a great part in the life of the western world. Taking Christ's words to the letter, he insisted upon the fact that it is only through the shedding of all earthly goods and possessions that one can free the spirit. In his world, men are not only brothers among themselves, they are also brothers to the animal and vegetable kingdom, and the road to Heaven is lit by universal love and must go through the rejection of all material attachments. This not only opened the way to the great mystics, but also to Dante's rise to Paradise through the true mediation of the ideal love of a woman, right up to the essence of the feminine, the Holy Virgin. An atmosphere of peace, repose and equilibrium seems to descend upon the western world. Art passes from the contortions and baroque exuberance of the Romanesque to the purity of lines and fluid, musical grace of the Gothic which, born in France, soon spread to England and to other parts of Europe. In England, it took, as all things do, a flavour of its own. Paris was the great centre of learning, where one could meet at the same time Thomas Aquinas, Albert the Great, Roger Bacon, Duns Scotus and, a little later, William of Ockham.

These three last named great thinkers herald, with Thomas Aquinas, the full growth of rationalism in the western world. Roger Bacon and Ockham were English-born, and Duns Scotus was, of course, a Scot. Roger Bacon advocated experimentalism on one side and intuitive or revelatory knowledge on the other. He obviously anticipates Locke. Duns Scotus maintained the Platonic, Augustinian leanings of Anselm and John Salisbury, and William of Ockham, the most important philosopher since Thomas Aquinas, is both a continuation of the previous philosophers, who blended mysticism and rationalism, and the point at which idealistic rationalism and experimental rationalism meet. On the one hand, he insists on the fact that understanding is of things and not of forms of the mind, and that experiment and facts are the basis of knowledge—something which leads straight to Francis Bacon and Locke. On the other hand, he says: "to prove a proposition is to demonstrate that it is immediately evident, or can be deduced from one which is immediately evident", and this is something which leads straight to Descartes. For Ockham, knowledge always presupposes perceptual knowledge of individual things and is therefore experimental. This experimentalism, which is basic to English thought, and which, as will be seen later, is at the roots of materialism, was a great incentive to the study of physics and astronomy in both countries, and obviously to the great discoveries which were soon to come into being in the fifteenth century.

So it can easily be seen that up to the end of the Hundred Years' War, which was a dynastic and feudal war between Plantagenets and Capetians and Valois, and between Armagnacs and Burgundians, all trying to weld France and England into one single kingdom, the meshes which united the English and French people were such that they held them together as members of the same warring family. Those who had the means to do so, lived well, travelled and prayed God that He might bless their wealth and good life; those who, alas, had to live like beasts in the woods or slaves in wealthy domains, prayed God that He might reward their earthly hell with His own longed-for heaven. And it was in those far-off days that we really had the first sample of Franco-British co-operation, a kind of "Concorde Project" in literature, *Le Morte d'Arthur*.

V

Languages

Once France and England decided, in spite of the Plantagenets, to be two separate Kingdoms and two separate nations, and once the English language became, with Chaucer, the official literary language of England, the way was open for differentiations in thought and feelings, and political and social developments which came to underlie some of the differences in culture between the two countries. These differences, for what they are, seem to rest, above all, first upon the fact that Britain is an island and France a crossroad, where everyone can peacefully or forcefully come and go. This is a way of saying that the geographical situation of these two countries has impinged considerably on their political structure and history. Secondly, there is the fact that each nation has its own language which, although closely related to the other, has developed differently, and has therefore played an important part in the moulding of the thought, sensibility and politico-social structure of the country to which it belongs. A language is a living whole which embodies and reflects the essential traits of the people who gave it life, fashioned it and use it. The English language is a richer and more flexible language than the French; therefore it seems to be a much better medium for poetry than the French. It is a strongly stressed language, something which easily facilitates the establishment of a given rhythm, without having to rely on a syllabic pattern, or on rhymes, which can advantageously be replaced by alliterations and assonances. Perhaps French would have been a more musical language if the *langue d'oc* had not been completely overwhelmed by the *langue d'oïl*. Probably due to its more complex origins—Germanic, Saxon, Latin, Norman, French—English has maintained a much greater flexibility in word-coinage, word groupings and in syntax than French, and it has a much wider vocabulary and a greater number of monosyllabic words, something which makes for a wide musical range. Above all, it has amalgamated a variety of rhythms which are the very basis of poetry, for poetry and the basic poetic emotion are, above all, rhythm and music. There is a rhythm of the Anglo-Saxon verse which constantly recurs throughout English poetry; there is the Celtic rhythm and the love of pattern and imagery which is the hallmark of poetry written by the Irish, Welsh and Scots, and there is also a certain syllabic rhythm which comes from the French and which was, and in an attenuated form still is, part of Irish poetry, and which is still alive in English poetry even today. The English word has, on the whole, more individuality than the French word, which is generally more abstract, more of an ideogram of the thing itself.

The English, being, on the whole, a pragmatic, utilitarian people more interested in action than in meditation, have developed a language which is admirably suited to convey action; 'on the whole' is the operative phrase, for England has produced remarkable mystics. The verb in English is the all-important word, and not only can most substantives be used as verbs, but ancillary words can be reduced to the bare minimum, so that one can come at once to the meaning expressed by the verb. Its grammar, if it is not quite like everything English, that is to say, pragmatic and *ad hoc*, is both flexible and simple in comparison with the rigidity and the complexity of the French. The French word has no specific accent or stress; all syllables have practically the same stress and must therefore be pronounced with the same care. All syllables are equal, as parts of the French constitution and of the French grammar. The one is, in principle, as orderly as the other. In linguistics, as everywhere else in French life, there are strict rules and they must be respected. In the French language there are no aristocrats to carry the stress; there is everywhere order, equality and fraternity. One cannot in French, as one can in English, begin a sentence with a preposition, such as 'down', or 'up', or what one likes. There must be logic, and logic requires that one should begin with the subject, so that one may know from the beginning what exactly to expect. Not so with English, in which the meaning may vary like the meanders of a river, according to the impact that the words as they come, produce upon the listener. 'Down went . . .' could be followed by 'the table', 'the president', 'the

king'—anything one likes. In French, one must know at once who
or what went down. In the same way, one cannot in French have
such syntactic arrangements as: "it is an elegant, well built, etc.
boat, home, young person", whatever one likes. The French toler-
ate a short adjective before the substantive, but a string of
adjectives—no! They must know from the start who or what is
going to carry them, and, once the substantive has been mentioned, one cannot, as in English, keep up the suspense and give
unexpected ends to sentences.

The French love mental order but they are politically unruly;
the English are mentally pragmatic, taking things as they come,
but they are politically co-operative. Their respective languages
express these two different attitudes and also contribute to their
making. So do, up to a point, their respective educational systems.
The French learn how to write a dissertation which has a beginning, a carefully balanced argument, and an end. The English learn
how to write essays, that is to say, they learn how to express themselves freely and spontaneously on a given subject. They are not
trained in the surgical art of dissecting and analysing a text, just
as until recently they were not trained in the art of cooking,
although they love both good cooking and a good text. But they
have countless debating and literary societies in which they practise the art of public debate and oratory. The French put a greater
stress than the English on the study of the classics, the humani-
ties and the art of rhetoric, which applies to writing as well as to
diction. The English distrust rhetoric, even though they have produced some of the greatest masters of it, Churchill being the last.
The French are masters of rhetoric, and, notwithstanding M. Revel,
who cannot possibly believe that he is the only one qualified to
award golden apples, De Gaulle's mastery of style and eloquence
offer some of the high watermarks of French prose and rhetoric.

French prosody rests mainly on a syllabic pattern, the music
of the vowels, which is extremely varied, intonations, pitch and
pauses, meant to convey meaning, and on rhyme, which helps to
underline the structure of the verse and to counteract a fluidity
of speech which tends naturally towards eloquence. English, with
its concreteness, its suggestiveness, musicality and ambiguity of
meaning, tends more naturally towards poetry than towards the
clearcut meanings of prose. Here one must, of course, be careful,

and not jump to conclusions, for it would be sheer heresy to suggest, or even to hint at, the notion that English is not a good medium for prose and that it does not contain masterpieces in prose. That is a suggestion which is not even worth refuting; no one in his senses would think of making it. The prose of Burke, Gibbon, Macaulay, Hume, Churchill, and that of the great English novelists compares favourably with the prose of any other literature. But the point I am trying to make is, first, that French being more than English an analytical language, with a more limited vocabulary and a far more rigid syntax, requires the skill of genius to be masterly handled in poetry. Great poetry can be written in it, as great as any in the world. The works of Villon, Ronsard, Racine, Baudelaire or Hugo are there to prove this point, but when the poetry is mediocre, it is far more mediocre than mediocre English poetry, simply because the language offers less natural help. Secondly, French prose reached full growth and maturity before English prose, and it is safe to say that while nothing in France compares with the poetry of Shakespeare, nothing in England compares, at that same time, with the prose of Rabelais, Montaigne, Pascal or of Descartes, and this in spite of the individual greatness and importance of Bacon. The point of this argument is not to establish orders of pre-eminence among poets or prose writers, a very useless pastime, but to show the important rôle played by language in the making of the genius or culture of any given country. Again, one must not read into this remark an exact relationship of cause and effect, and therefore conclude that a given language always produces a given effect. Such conclusions can be obtained in laboratory work, but not when dealing with the live interplay of language and thought and sensibility. The two terms, language and artistic expression, are closely related; they certainly influence one another, but to try to see with certainty which one is subsumed under the other is to try to solve the unsolvable problem of the egg and the hen. One can only note the differences which have been suggested and attempt a phenomenological description of the facts, in order to see how far these differences exist in reality.

VI

Renaissance and Sixteenth Century

The word Renaissance is generally taken to refer to the great revival of the arts, and consequently of western human sensibility, which took place in the great cities of Northern Italy, and later in Europe, from the second half of the fourteenth century, throughout the fifteenth and the early sixteenth. This revival is supposed to have taken place under the influence of classical models from Greece and Rome. That this is rather an oversimplification of the rise and fall of human activities, spiritual or otherwise, there is no doubt. For human changes are always evolutionary, that is to say, they never begin at a given moment and end in a clearcut fashion at another. Being in every case the result of deep-rooted and fully integrated historical causes, social and artistic changes neither begin at an unarguable given date nor are they confined to one single, self-contained manifestation. There are, strictly speaking, no radical mutations in the field of historical developments, any more than there are mutations in the domain of physics, in spite of the principle of indeterminacy which only applies to infinitesimally small particles, and which, in fact, could well be considered of purely temporary value, until further experiments and discoveries have proved that their apparent unpredictability in behaviour introduced by, or at any rate connected with, the presence of the observer is abolished by some necessary corrective, which restores to the affected particles their normal basically determined behaviour within the organic structure to which they belong. Even in the domain of biology, mutational changes take place within the context of evolutionary heredity, and the chance mutations which are part of evolution, and those which may or may not have been the causes of the origins of life, could very well be described as due to chance, simply because they are part of a causality whose roots we can no longer explore, nor will ever be able to explore;

for one only becomes aware of the intervention of what we call chance, that is to say, of unexplained causality, once the event which it causes has taken place, and therefore once this event has resolved and absorbed its causality, whatever it may have been, into itself. This argument, which might appear to some as abstruse or recondite, and perhaps to others even as out of place, is, in fact, not so, and is to the contrary here stated as being a basis for firm repudiation of the existence of clearcut movements and counter-movements in history and in art. There has been a Renaissance, there has been a Romantic Age, this is agreed, but these terms are only valid when applied to loosely defined historical periods. The Renaissance can no more be made to begin in 1453, with the fall of Constantinople to the Turks, than Romanticism can be made to begin in 1798, with the *Lyrical Ballads*. Giotto in Italy, the Master of Rheims Cathedral in France, were as much parts of a renaissance of the arts in their time as were Blake and Robert Burns parts of Romanticism, and, no doubt, the most fallacious way of describing these various artists is to apply to them the title of precursors to a given movement, ancestors, fathers, etc., as if artistic and social developments were a matter of progenitors, pedigrees, clearcut labels and prizes.

We all know what is generally meant by the Renaissance, but we must firmly do away with the notion that the Dark Ages and, least of all, the Middle Ages were barren, God-forsaken periods of the life of mankind in which men groped around, plagued by famine and disease, and unable ever to lift their gaze upwards or to apply their minds and skills to the task of inspiring and carrying forth the progress of the human condition. The age of St. Augustine, of the rise of Mahometan civilization, which brought Greece and the East in contact with the western world, cannot be looked upon as a blighted period of the life of mankind. Least of all could the age of the Carolingians, of Alcuin, of Charlemagne and his education programme, be looked upon as a recessive or dark age in the life of man.

Although any examination of Franco-British relations could hardly ignore 1066 and the arrival of the Normans in Great Britain, the end of that century is certainly marked by a great reawakening of activity in all aspects of human life. It is the beginning of the Crusades, the perfect illustration of the truth of the dictum that the road to heaven is paved with very unchristian intentions, for what could be more unchristian than the misguided belief that the best way of implementing the Sermon on the Mount is by killing off those of our fellow beings who worship God in ways different from ours? This belief has had, alas, a long innings in the life of Christian Europe; in fact, it still applies now against so-called 'red' heretics. But, intentions apart, the Crusades did not only bring to the West cherries and silks; they also brought back some of the wisdom of the East, while they somehow took with them, and left behind, some of that urgent energy, which, with the exception of a few smouldering periods apart, has, from Socrates onward, kept the western world on the march in quest of the ever increasing fruits of reason. The twelfth and thirteenth centuries not only saw the splendid blossoming of Romanesque art, particularly in France, but also the rise of Gothic art in the Ile-de-France, the re-emergence of aspects of classicism which blended with Romanesque, and also, as part of this interest in classicism, the awakening of humanism, with philosophers of the calibre of John of Salisbury and Abélard, whose humanism and aversion to scholasticism called forth upon them the suspicion and hostility of the Church.

By the end of the thirteenth century, scholasticism had gained the upper hand, the classical influences were progressively discarded, while Romanesque art was more and more replaced by Gothic art, rationalism was taking wings with William of Ockham and Thomas Aquinas, and poetry was about to reach unsurpassed heights with Dante. By the end of the fourteenth century, Gothic art was in full blossom and the influence of the classical arts had once more receded, even in Italy. By the beginning of the fifteenth century, French, Flemish and Dutch art, which were the dominant arts at that time, turned their attention more and more towards the apprehension of the reality of their age. Whether this was due to the great social upheavals and suffering caused by the ravages of the Black Death, by the endless wars spread all over Europe, by the first loosening of the church's influence on life, or, above all, by the rise of rationalism, is something difficult to say. The fact is that the paintings of Jan Van Eyck, and of most of the great Flemish masters, as well as the poetry of Villon, the greatest poet of the age, face up to the reality of their time. Their stark, clearcut imagery, shorn of any conceptual comments, describe the horrors, the misery and the nobility of life, and beyond the lure of the senses, one can see the shadows of the dancing daemons, or the redemptory heaven where much harrowed and tormented man might find, in the end, peace. Creation at that time is still informed with God's subsistent presence, and man is only aware of his true existence in as far as he feels connected with God. Some of the poetry of Chaucer in *The Canterbury Tales* and particularly the poetry of Robert Henryson in *The Testamend of Cresseid*, a masterpiece, partake of this same stark realism. The Scots, from Henryson and Dunbar to Burns, have always shown a strong sense of realism in poetry, and few poetic creations are more moving than scabs-covered Cresseid, mourning, unrecognized by her former lover, at the gates of Troy. Nowhere are realism, satirical and Rabelaisian exuberance, better illustrated than in Dunbar's *The Dance of the Seven Deidlie Synnis*. His fantasy and boisterousness anticipate Burns, and his famous *Lament for the Makaris* has echoes of Villon, whose work Dunbar must have known during his bohemian life in Paris.

Side by side with this widespread concern for reality, there is at that time a revival of neo-platonism unparalleled since the twelfth century translation of the Pseudo-Areopagite, by John the Scot, and the philosophy of the Abbé Suger. This neo-platonism, far from following Plato's advice of banning the poet out of the city, saddles him and other artists with the task of providing guidance to the rest of mankind. With this neo-platonism, the barrier between the sacred and the profane is abolished, and its influence is strongly felt in the poetry of the age, from the *Pléiade* in France to Italian and English poetry or the writings of Erasmus. What is interesting is that in Italy the flowering of the arts expressed itself mostly in painting and in sculpture, Christian in theme and subject, yet looking back to Greece in appearances and shapes, while in France and in England, the best flowering was in poetry, lyric poetry in France, dramatic poetry in England where it reached, with Shakespeare, its golden age. Yet, of course, one should not stress too much the difference between these two manifestations of art, for Leonardo da Vinci has wisely declared: "Painting is poetry that can be seen". Still, this being said, the cleavage between the art of Italy, on the one side, and that of England and France, on the other, was far wider than Da Vinci's generalization could possibly suggest. The paintings and sculptures of the Italian Renaissance, at least those which had religious themes and subjects, and these were by far the largest number, were, in one respect, not unlike the cathedrals which had been built earlier. These paintings and sculptures had Greek appearances and they were composed so as to be 'measured by Greek standards, but they were, like the cathedrals, expressions of the Christian faith, and, as such, they were meant to call forth feelings of piety, admiration and respect for the Divinity. They were, in many ways, acts of worship, and they were in any case an expression of man's sense of humility and of his wretched loneliness without the Grace of the infinite Majesty who has created him and who carefully weighs every one of his earthly actions in order to decide whether He will take him to His bosom or reject him. Even the portraits or the landscape paintings of the aforementioned masters have about them this aura of unfathomable mystery and distance between the real and the ideal which characterizes, on the whole, Renaissance art. I say 'on the whole' for, although these traits were the dominant aspects of art, there were other aspects too. Life at that time was not entirely looked upon as a homage to God through Greek patterns and structures. Life could also be looked upon as being fragmented and made of striking contrasts which blended violence, passion and suffering with attitudes of total indifference. While, for instance, the Flagellation takes place in the painting of that name by Piero della Francesca, the figures in the foreground stare blankly in front of them, and they look as totally unconcerned by what happens about them as the ploughman in Brueghel's *Fall of Icarus*.

Things were different with the arts of France and of England. True enough, the poetry of the *Pléiade* teems with Gods, Goddesses, nymphs and hamadryads. Yet, although Ronsard, the master of all was a church canon, his poetry, whatever it is, is not a homage to God; it is rather a desperate cry that life is short and that therefore, while man must do what he can with its brevity and with the possibility which it offers, he must also think of the soul, yet only in due time. What is interesting at that time is that the Attic light and the Attic models, though still present, fade faster and faster away, until both in painting and in the dramatic poetry of England man turns his gaze squarely and fully upon reality, joining forces with the steady gaze of Van Eyck or of Villon, who had looked at life in the light of God, certainly, but also as it was, that is to say, carrying with it such a continuous, ever present stench of decay that no foam-bathed thyme-perfumed Cytherean Venus could hide or wish it away. This attitude marks the return to one of the two aspects of realism, the one which, instead of looking at reality through the prism of the Greek ideal form, which is the ideal of the Divine transferred through Greek influence to Christianity, on the contrary looks at reality as the phenomenal appearance of an ideal or essence, which the creative imagination can reach and suggest through its subjectively caught phenomenality. This being so, the attempt to exclude from realism idealization, which is a necessary part of subjectivity in art, is purely and simply an illusion, or an attempt to confine realism to an impossible imitation of the slice of life, and generally a low slice of life. Neither St. Augustine nor St. Thomas, who was a realist, committed this error. Every type of true art is both realistic and idealistic. It is idealistic in the sense that it unavoidably contains aspects, more or less marked, of the essential vision of the artist, and it is realistic in the sense that it represents or exteriorizes more or less important social forces of the age to which it belongs, and a more or less objective representation of perennial reality. If reality is felt as purely subjective and deprived of any objective value, the representative element will, as is the case at this moment in time, be practically non-existent and it will then be replaced by mental constructions. Delacroix, who knew and could talk about painting better than any painter ever did, thought that David was a strange blend of realism and idealism, though less idealistic than Rembrandt but as idealistic as Raphael, whose imitations of reality were at times more faithful than those of David.

In his way, Da Vinci is both as realistic and idealistic as Rembrandt. He gives us the reality of his age, and that reality consisted in seeing human beings, including Biblical characters, in terms of Greek figures which are the logos through which they commune with eternity. For, although St. Anne, the Holy Virgin, John the Baptist and the Mona Lisa have all something in common (they all cast back to the Greek world), the tremors of inner reality which break through their features are, in each case, the manifestations of the individual essence of what they are intended to be and are and which relate them to Eternity, to which they belong as much as to their time. The various heads of Rembrandt are also realistic and idealistic; they contain both the head of a given human being and an idealization of the essence which animates him or her, and it is this idealization which relates, for instance, the head of the Prodigal Son to other heads in his paintings and to some of his self-portraits. It is nearly always the same head, that of Man face to face with Christ, representative of mankind's suffering. Da Vinci also somehow nearly always paints the same woman's head, but he idealizes the form or appearance, which becomes essentialized into an ideal; while Rembrandt particularizes the appearance and endeavours to bring out the essence of each particular, something which is also a form of idealization. What matters for a religious man is God, and Rembrandt was a religious man. Whatever face he painted, he always searched for the same, ever unchanging thing—the essence of man in the presence of his Maker. Beyond idealism, or beyond the naturalistic representation of the illusion of the appearance, his quest was always that of all the great masters and creative minds, the quest for the Absolute. The interplay of light and darkness, the spirituality which emanates from each of his characters, bind them all together, in the same way as the interplay of light and darkness, of hope, and despair, of angelic flights, purgatorial urges and sense of ineluctable destiny, bind together all the great characters of Shakespeare. Shakespeare and Rembrandt! How close they are, and also how different they are from Racine or from Corneille, who, if they were not absolutely contemporaries of Shakespeare, were contemporaries of Rembrandt, of Vermeer and of Rubens.

Shakespeare was born the very year when Michelangelo died, and it is, above all, with Rembrandt and Michelangelo that lie the affinities of his genius. Although classical allusions and influences abound in his work, in just the same way as thirteenth-century Gothic art had absorbed them, they have become, through the imagination of his universal genius, organic parts of creations which defy any attempt to track down influences, similarities, or groupings. These creations are certainly not standing in a vacuum, but they stand on their own, they are part of life, and they reach back and forth beyond their ages into the timeless and the world, wherever men may live. No doubt some of his French contemporaries such as Garnier, Hardy, Montaigne and Rabelais can claim affinities with him, to say nothing of metaphysical poets, like Maurice Scève and Louise Labé, whose neo-platonism, love of conceit and refinements of rhetoric find echoes in Shakespeare's sonnets as well as in Spenser's. But it is above all with Montaigne's humanism, Rabelais's luxuriant life and wisdom, together with the works of Garnier and Hardy that Shakespeare's affinities lie. Garnier's use of the chorus and his blending of the tragic and lyricism, as in *Les Juives*, and Hardy's fertility of imagination and range of actions and emotions, transcending literary genius and places, clearly show that, although it happened the way it did, French drama might not have culminated, as it did, in the type of drama created by Racine and Corneille. It is, on the other hand, true that Garnier's blend of rhetoric and biblical passion heralds both. Nevertheless, what determined the fate of French drama lies undeniably in the ascendancy assumed by classical studies and models, as well as other aspects of academic learning. Enthusiasm for learning, and, of course, for pedantry and the love of rules, was spreading, and every educated person knew or claimed to know about the so-called Aristotelian rules of drama; and if one adds to this quasi-ubiquitous knowledge of the rules the widespread regard of the majority of French people for systems and categories, one can understand why the neo-classical drama of De La Taille and Jodelle triumphed over that of Garnier and Hardy and opened the way to Racine and Corneille, thus parting company with Elizabethan drama.

The reasons for this are above all social; the times have changed. The Elizabethan age is an age during which the transition between ancient feudalism and rising metropolitan life comes to an end. The individualism of the Renaissance is still active, manifesting itself in discoveries, explorations and adventures in far-flung countries. Imagination is still an integral part of a society which has shaken off the shackles of old dominations and is full of self-confidence. In spite of Francis Bacon, reason has not yet become the predominant faculty of the mind. On the other hand, the age of Racine and Corneille is dominated by King and religion, and reason has gained the ascendancy. The theatre is no longer a representation of reality apprehended as a whole by imagination, but an illusion of reality organized according to the preoccupations, the desires and the dreams of a society concerned not with all-embracing explorations and changes in all domains, but with the happenings of the human heart and conscience, expounded according to the rules and conventions. The theatre of Shakespeare is a microcosm of social life in his time, and, through the archetypal qualities of his main characters, in historical time. He does not attempt to produce an illusion of reality or an apparently veridic sequence of events conforming to time and place. The imagination easily embraces all sorts of actions taking place simultaneously on a multi-levelled stage, and is no way bothered by the sight of one king fast asleep in his tent while his enemy, the other king, is seen marching towards him. The Italian-style stage, which became the classical stage and has dominated the European theatre, including England, for over two centuries, precludes such a range of simultaneous actions. In fact, small, overcrowded with spectators on the sides, it offered hardly any room for any action whatsoever. This rejection of action was obviously part of the sensibility of the public. Action in the classical theatre, comedy excepted, is always in the past or in the future, but not in the present, for it is neither welcome by a society which prefers intellectual reflection and decorum to kinetic displays, nor easy on a restricted stage. Time or the notion of time has changed. Medieval, Renaissance and Elizabethan time can be said to be synchronic, all-embracing, and still connected with transcendence. Seventeenth-century time is diachronic, sequential; it is continuous creation out of nothingness. Descartes, Pascal and Calvin, whether they hang this creation on God's grace or on the negativity of the mind, all reflect this precarious aspect of man's life and salvation. Reality has become internal, psychological and based on conscience. Therefore language is all, and it is either used as a means of rational domination in the theatre of Corneille or as the instrument which reveals and brings death in the theatre of Racine.

The Scottish "makars" had affinities with poets like Du Bartas and D'Aubigné, whose imagination, passion, disdain for rules, strength and genuineness of feelings are, with the exception of Hugo's poetry in *Les Châtiments*, more attuned to Protestant English sensibility than to the dominant French sensibility. It is not without reason that du Bartas's great poem was translated in English as soon as it was published, and that it achieved a much greater reputation in England than in France. It prefigures Milton, who found in it comfort and encouragement for his own great epic.

D'Aubigné also had affinities with Milton, but he lacked the English poet's genius to control his material and to lift theology above the coarse passion of street fights and public arena quarrels, and to see conflict *sub specie aeternitatis*. One does not know whether or not Shakespeare knew of, or read, Rabelais, but whether he did so or not, there is no doubt that Rabelais, whose scepticism and avoidance of extremes are typically French, exhibits also some traits which show close affinities with the English genius. His Falstaffian humour, his directness, copiousness of details and straightforward lack of self-consciousness are all part of the love for, and faith in, nature and in what is called the 'natural', which plays such a part in Shakespeare, particularly in *King Lear*. His jocularity and satire about monks had been anticipated by Chaucer's *Canterbury Tales*, but there is no doubt that Panurge could easily find a place in Shakespeare's histories and comedies. Rabelais's total lack of concern for form is in direct contrast with the aesthetics of the members of the *Pléiade* and with those of Malherbe who, in some ways, completes the *Pléiade*, and who standing at the close of the sixteenth century and at the opening of the seventeenth, illustrates in poetry a form of conceptualism and concern for rules and formal polish which mark the beginning of quite important differences of approach between English and French art. It is therefore all the more important to note that besides Ronsard, the *Pléiade* comprises poets like Du Bellay who had remarkable affinities with English artistic sensibility. His wistful pantheism, his melancholy and nostalgic longing for his homeland, his love of nature, closely akin to English romanticism or to the poetry of Vaughan, his Keatsian intimations of an early death, and his staunch love of animals, are all parts of a poetry which is not very remote from traditional English poetry. We may reproach him or, at least, tease him about his *Défense de la Langue Française*, which has anticipated the *Parlez-vous Franglais* of Etiemble, though it must be said that his purpose was purely didactic. Ronsard, undeniably the greatest poet of his time save Shakespeare, has written elegies and sonnets which stand

71

comparison with Shakespeare's. The famous sonnet which teased
Yeats into paraphrasing it, as well as others addressed to Cassandra, Hélène, Marie, Queen Elizabeth I, and Mary Queen of
Scots, are among the best that have ever been written. From
Horace's defiance to mortality, to Shakespeare, Marvell or Donne,
nobody has expressed this theme better than Ronsard in the famous
sonnet, beginning with the words: *"Quand vous serez bien
vieille."*

VII

Seventeenth Century

The thought that the seventeenth century begins in 1600 carries
no more truth than the old debated and counter-debated statement: *"Enfin—ou hélas—Malherbe vint!"* Malherbe, the pedant
laureate, whose only genius was patience and self-assurance, is
merely an effect and not a cause, a feeble tune in a vast orches-
tration whose dominant themes began to emerge in the 1630s
with the creation of the *Académie* by Richelieu and with the
publication of Descartes' first great work in 1637, which was the
year after the first production of *Le Cid*. The separation of creation
from transcendence, which had taken place at the end of the
Middle Ages, is on the whole continued by the separation of man
from nature. The fluctuating thought of Montaigne is not connected
to anything and is a continuous question-mark. With Descartes,
thought withdrawn from temporality endeavours to reach, through
a kind of intellectual ascesis, a moment of pure intuition, which is
proof of existence and which corresponds to the initial act of
creation. This moment of intuition, which links time and eternity,
is a pure act of mind transcending time and implying neither continuity nor contact between matter and spirit; therefore Being is
no longer continuous, as in the Catholic Middle Ages, but merely
confined to the instant which has to be continuously repeated.
The awareness of the fleetingness of life is increased and becomes
a source of great anxiety for all except the stoics or staunch believers in will of the Cornelian type. For those who believe in
God, creation requires the continuous renewal of God's grace;
thence the anxiety of those who, deprived of predestinarian beliefs,
know that, however just they may be, all might be lost without
actual grace. The Pascalian moment of grace, born from nakedness,
anxiety, void and faith in God's mercy, echoes the *cogito* of Descartes, reached through willed nothingness; Racine's Phèdre, a

73

Jansenist like Pascal, is a sinner who did not receive grace; quietists and active Catholics had a similar feeling of anxiety and dependence upon God's grace. We have, therefore, either immanence without transcendence for those who believe in will, or transcendence connected with temporality through grace or intuition in moments which transcend time.

The end of the spiritual and physical upheavals of the Renaissance and Reformation, and the emergence of strong national rulers, such as Elizabeth I in England and Richelieu in France, imply also the emergence of a new sensibility. The spirit of individualism and adventure gives way slowly to a strongly hierarchized society which, whether in religion or in politics, believes in respect for the established rules. This new society, having acquired learning, wealth and leisure, requires a new form of entertainment which bear-baiting, cock-fighting or minstrels can no longer provide. Neither can religious drama continue to satisfy the artistic longings of men who either condemn the theatre as a hotbed of sin or are more and more inclined to uphold the separation between the temporal and the spiritual. The growth of metropolitan life centred on the court called for a social form of entertainment; the theatre was the answer, and the poet the man to provide it. Until then, the poet had been a myth-maker, a singer, a servant of faith or an interpreter of the mysteries of the universe; from now on, he can still fill all those parts according to his genius and beliefs, but he must, above all, entertain. He may be a poet by vocation, but society expects him to be a professional entertainer and to "please" in return for honour and wealth. Religious or political discussions in art are out of place; they are part of the ruler's prerogative, and as such are beyond the scope of the poet. Overt moralizing or display of personal feelings are bad manners in the age of respect for conventions and of *l'honnête homme*. The poet performs his task without trying to singularize himself by literary revolutions or ostentatious poses. The only fitting pose he can adopt is that of *magister*, upholder of order, like Malherbe, or *législateur du Parnasse*, like Boileau.

Not so in England, and this is the time when differences between English and French cultures began to assert themselves, though, of course, without undue excesses and, least of all, without any possibilities of the type of clearcut categorizations which have made the delight of some historians of literature. After the long protracted debates about the importance of rules and canons of artistic achievements based on the ancients, France did not suddenly adopt wholeheartedly these rules, and did not set about producing only classical or neo-classical works. Far from it; all sorts of trends and aspects of art and artistic manifestations survived in the midst of this rising classical art. The romantic tendencies, the passion and violence of the poetry of Du Bartas and D'Aubigné were no doubt slowly swamped by the rising urgency for control and good manners, which characterized *l'honnête homme* of the seventeenth century, not to be confused with the English gentleman, who is more humane, more ethically minded than his well-equilibrated, intellectually controlled French counterpart.

Racan and Maynard, Malherbe's friends and followers, have much greater gifts, Maynard particularly, without nevertheless transcending the boundaries of minor poetry. With him, more than with Malherbe, emerges a certain Villonesque realism about the decay of the body, the cruelty of age and of death unredeemed by any pagan Elysium, which connects him with the nineteenth century. But a poet who shows greater stature and more variety in his poetry than any of the School of Malherbe is Saint-Amant. His exuberance, his verbal skill and range of moods, from passionate, ribald, Verlainian bohemianism to the holy fervour of his last years, link him up with the Romantics, who, through Gautier and Rémy de Gourmont, hailed him as an ancestor and gave him a high place in seventeenth-century non-dramatic poetry. He can be truly realistic and macabre in an age which only represents death in the apparel of greatness, and he shows a genuine love of nature and solitude, something rather rare in his age, except in the works of Théophile de Viau and in those of La Fontaine, who, for that and other reasons, incurred the displeasure of Boileau.

In diction La Fontaine breaks all the rules imposed by Malherbe and Boileau; his language is racy, subtle, and varying in tone according to the characters involved; his line is flexible, suited to the effect he is aiming at, and overflowing whenever necessary. His wit, his imagery, his gifts of observation about human and animal behaviour, and his innate sense of drama, make of him a wonder-painter of the life of his time and a *raconteur* worthy to stand beside the greatest. His bland *bonhomie* and his use of apologues enable him to satirize and to deal with problems which were obviously very much in men's minds, but which were made taboo by the authorities. His reputation is solid outside France and in France, of which he is with Molière perhaps the most perfect representative. He forms a *genre* by himself; one could not call him a great poet, for his work lacks some of the fundamental prerequisites which make great poetry, yet he has a genuine lyrical vein, and his technical skill and intellectual and affective range are those of a great writer. Molière is the most outstanding universal genius which France has produced. The *genre* in which he worked, comedy, well separated in France from tragedy, does not elicit much poetry, though there are in his plays numerous moments of poignant irony and great pathos. He used verse as part of the conventions of the age, but his genius lies in the revelation of character and situations which, through his vision, acquire universal significance.

The two most important poet-dramatists which France has produced are Racine and Corneille. The garb of similar conventions which both wear hides fundamental differences, which render inane any attempt to see the work of the one as a continuation of the other. The world of Corneille is the world of the immanence of the human will, which makes itself in a continuous present beyond good and evil and which becomes transcendent. Whether struggling for life or moving towards death, the Cornelian hero remains master of himself and of the universe, and, with his superhuman will, he reaches the instant which defies time. He can say: "I will therefore I am." The dramatic action feeds the will, which can only be known in action; but one always knows that whatever the challenge, the response will be there, and even when the hero bemoans his fate, as Rodrigue and Polyeucte do, one is aware that the song is, in the main, a convention or an aside of the hero whose will cannot break and whose reward on earth or in Heaven is certain. Words in Corneille are a means to an end, which is conviction; they have no internal resonance, they are part of a passionate rhetoric showing greater skill, greater verbal virtuosity than that of any other French dramatist; they dazzle, they stun, but they do not create experience, for they are part of a world which precludes it because of its lack of truly religious depth. The world of Racine is a religious world, a world in which transcendence connects with time through grace or at the point of death, when the hero, about to lose life, realizes the extent to which his sinful presence corrupts light or causes agony to God. By then, it is always too late, for knowledge is ever the irreversible past, and once the hero realizes the distance which separates him from God, death is the only gesture, for death is his true destiny and the only possible means of returning to the whole. The action here is not a piling up of incidents in order to increase tension towards the *dénouement*, but a ruthless shedding of illusions and hopes through words, which do not protect or save but, as in true tragedy, whether Greek or Christian, reveal to the hero the extent of his misfortune and the gaping grave at his feet; they do not feed and defend life or a transcendent will; they kill, that is to say, they perform their true poetic function: they return the individual to death, the great source of creation. After this oblation by words, after these ethereal pyres from which strange superhuman characters rise like phoenixes through immortal songs, nothing remains; the radioactive substances of the words and of the rhythms of French poetry have been exhausted, and here I agree with Thierry Maulnier that *"si Racine avait eu des héritiers, il n'eût point été complétement Racine. . . ."* Once an action or an aspect of creation has reached its apex, its classical moment, it can only be followed by a period of sterility, which, in France, lasted for approximately 150 years.

Richelieu's authoritarian rule had curbed the individualism of the Renaissance and of the Reformation which, having failed to win the support of the monarchy, had little chance of success in France. Henri IV had wisely decided that Paris was well worth a mass, and although his assassination in 1610 sparked off new disturbances and disorders, Richelieu soon succeeded in putting down rebellions and in decimating the aristocracy, which was compelled to learn more and more the lesson that the only way to prosper and to gather favour from the King or the ruler of the day, was through pliability and constant presence at court. This led the nobles into deserting more and more their country estates and into a widening gap between them and their tenants or employees; more importantly, it resulted in the total destruction of the power of a class which, until then, had been able to question and to counterbalance the King's authority. The King found himself more and more isolated at the top of a social and political pyramid, surrounded by acquiescent, profiteering courtiers, and completely insulated from the suffering and plight of his oppressed people, who, in the end, could only make their grievances felt through revolution. After the brief interlude of the *Fronde*, Louis XIV ascended the throne and with a firm hand he answered the longing of the French people for order and internal peace, and during sixty years of absolute rule over a hierarchized society through his direct influence, the influence of the court, the Academy and the public, everything combined to keep the arts each to its separate *genre* and conventions.

Although there are certain similarities between the political and social developments of England and France, in the sense that in England there was also, during the first half of the seventeenth century, a strong authoritarian rule alternating with revolutions until the end of the Stuarts and the Restoration, the arts in England retained their complete independence and their *sui generis* nature. Owing to the King's intervention, the Reformation won the day in England, and with the end of the Stuarts this success took, practically for good, every kind of religious acrimony and bitterness out of political life. At least, it is more or less so in the British Isles, with the exception of Northern Ireland and parts of Scotland. Whether due to the French passion for ideas and ideology or to the fact that the aborted Reformation transferred on to political life a good deal of religious frustration, the truth is that French politics have carried, from the Great Revolution onwards, a fervour and divisiveness which could only be described as religious.

No amount of renewal of studies of ancient arts and literature, no lengthy discussion of Aristotle's rules, could succeed in persuading English poets and artists to conform to them. There was, in England, no Academy to add its weight to these pressures, and the public, educated or otherwise, did not long for such conformity. The English are conformist in politics and ethics, but are nonconformist in aesthetics and, by and large, in religion. Genius is, of course, essentially nonconformist and non-academic, and that being so, it is difficult to decide the importance played by the fact that, at the moment when the Renaissance was in full blossom in France and in England, France had no genius of Shakespeare's stature. On the other hand, one must take into consideration the fact that genius not only expresses the universal and the timeless, but also the historical moment and certain aspects of the ethos of the people to which he belongs. Therefore, one must be led to the conclusion that Shakespeare could only have been born in England, and also that, through him, are revealed some of the aspects of what could be called, broadly speaking, the English genius. Conformity to the laws of its own nature, rather than conformity to concepts and rules, is certainly one of its characteristics as far as art is concerned. By and large, shunning the attempt to conform to conventions and to rules, the best of English poetry has, on the contrary, generally endeavoured to conform to nature and to reality. As far as any social explanation of this attitude could be suggested, it must be said that French society from the seventeenth century onwards, whether it was part of the court or of the bourgeoisie, had generally endeavoured to play a greater part and to influence and to dictate the orientation of the arts to an extent completely unknown in English society. Therefore, up to a point, one can see why a very conventional and, in many ways, superficial society like early eighteenth century French society required, and was presented with, a very conventional art, which, as such, and in as far as this aspect of art corresponded to a given section of that society, found its reality in its relation to it. Using art as a means of assessment of the forces, ideals and vision latently at work in a given society, it seems possible to say that early eighteenth century French society was, in that part of it which was conscious of itself, rather superficial and without any deep core of human values, while that much larger and more important part, which was overburdened by material difficulties and afflicted by hopelessness, was practically amorphous and very little conscious of its own existence. Had art given expression to this situation, that part of society which was involved in it would have become conscious of its plight and would accordingly have been made able to alter it. When that moment came, with Rousseau and others, the Great Revolution was not far away.

Shakespeare, in common with Rembrandt, a genius of similar stature who was ten years old when the great English writer died, shows that artistic creativity cannot be governed by any external causes or models; it can only be governed by its own laws. The world of creativity is necessarily the world of the imagination, the world of Keats, Coleridge and Wordsworth, therefore a world sifted, absorbed and negated according to the creative forms which give shape and style to the material or the experience confronting the artist. It is neither Greek models nor other preconceived ideas which decide the structure of his work, but his vision, which, throughout his creative life, always decides practically automatically what he sees or does not see. Racine seems to be the coping-stone or the crown of his age. It is the same in some respects with Milton, while both Shakespeare and Rembrandt float above theirs and belong to all ages and to a world which stretches from the first Greek dramatists to Michelangelo and Da Vinci, whose greatest works like the *Pietà*, *Night* and *The Last Supper* show man face to face with his destiny and rising Christ-like above it. Rembrandt and Shakespeare reach beyond their age and are also part of it. Rembrandt expresses not only the longings, dreams and vision of perennial man, but also the ethos of the rich bourgeoisie of the Hanseatic League, self-satisfied, self-conscious about its power, yet also aware of the skeleton beyond the rosy, beguiling flesh and of the insignificant impression made by all wealth on the scales of divine justice. Rembrandt caught this divided world in immortal masterpieces. In a similar way, Shakespeare gave life to the experience of certain aspects of human kind, caught in England at that time between the crumbling down of an old world and the birth of a new one, with all the sorrows, suffering and redemptory joys that such moments of death and rebirth can entail. The early seventeenth century is an age of the rising ascendancy of science, of intoxicating discoveries opening new physical and mental horizons, an age which, rediscovering the old Pythagorean faith in numbers, tended to make of mathematics the basis of truth and knowledge, but which retained the belief that there is still greater truth in human experience and the imagination. Pascal, a mathematical genius worthy of the age of Descartes, Spinoza, Newton, Leibnitz, all great mathematicians, possessed, nevertheless, a metaphysical mind and an artistic sensibility which enabled him fully to understand, in spite of his denigrations of the imagination, that the truth that really matters is the truth of experience and of the heart. But there is no doubt that Pascal's voice, in France's classical age, was a minority voice. His uncompromising Christianity and his sensibility had more in common with that of his English contemporary, Milton, than with that of the court of Richelieu and Mazarin. He was not a great poet endowed with the epic and dramatic genius which enabled Milton to retell, in grandiose poetry, the creation and the fall of man, but he had the penetrating gaze of one of the most acute minds that ever was, and his picture of man face to face with his Maker is practically all light and no shadows, for as in Rembrandt's paintings the shadows are luminous; they are part of light.

If English and French seventeenth century arts take each their separate individual way—one towards conceptualism, which will exhaust itself, the other still bathing in imagination and experience, until it caught up with French conceptualism—in the Augustan age one witnesses the same parting of the ways in philosophy, and consequently in the underlying thought and sensibility of the two countries. Descartes, whose philosophy contains aspects of materialism which will acquire strength later, is primarily an idealistic rationalist. Instead of starting, like his great English contemporary, Bacon, from facts in order to arrive at laws, Descartes starts from the premise that the laws of the mind, which are the laws of mathematics, are the laws to which Nature must conform. We have here the crux of the difference between English and French cultures, a difference which is reflected both in the arts and in the political structures of the two countries. Cartesian philosophy leads both to eighteenth-century materialism and to the Hegelian notion that the rational is the real. The ideal, the world of the mind, is the structure in which one must endeavour to fit the facts. This is miles away from the *tabula rasa* notion of Locke or the empiricism of Bacon, and though one must concede with Kant, who is a kind of mediator between both theories, that the mind has structures and categories with which it carries out its storing up and its making of concepts and knowledge, it is a fact that the contrast between French idealistic rationalism and English empirical rationalism underlies throughout the cultures of the two countries, and is also one of the dialectical elements which played an important part in the making of the art and culture of Europe. Still the cleavage which separates Descartes' theories* of knowledge from English experimentalism and trust in perceptions must not make one forget the fact that Descartes, endowing matter with self-creative power through mechanical motion, is also one of the fathers of western materialism. In fact, materialism began with English philosophers like Duns Scotus and Ockham and, above all, with Bacon and Hobbes, but in due course French thought greatly contributed to it, and produced in the eighteenth century its own brand which was a blend of Cartesian and English materialism. Helvétius, La Mettrie and D'Holbach were responsible for the mixture of English and French materialism which returned to England to emerge with British Socialism, and which, in France, led straight to Socialism and Communism.

David Hume, 'le Bon David', who spent many years in France where he was greatly admired, is a Scotsman, and his introspectiveness, psychological interests and scepticism are more akin to French than to English thought. Bishop Berkeley was Irish, and his metaphysical preoccupations and idealism are more Celtic than English. His reduction of reality to mind found full support in Romantic subjectivism, and is obviously part of the trend which culminated in Hegelian idealism. Political philosophers and economists, whether they were Scots-born, like Adam Smith, or English-born, like Bentham, represent an important aspect of English thought, but none more so than Hobbes and Locke, who are not only basic to English thought, but also to the political evolution of the western world.

In 1637, the year when Descartes published his *Discours de la Méthode*, Hobbes, who was 49 years old, was in Paris, where he had many friends, for he had spent many years in France. He had already met Galileo, and he might even have been present at the performance of Corneille's first play *Le Cid*, which took place in 1636. A friend, and sometime secretary, of Francis Bacon, Hobbes was, like Descartes, primarily interested in mathematics, and his basic philosophical views are not unlike those of Descartes. "Philosophy," he said, "is such knowledge of effects and appearances as we acquire by true ratiocination from the knowledge we

---

* One must bear in mind, in connection with the French and Descartes, the fact that the word "theory" originally implied passionate, sympathetic contemplation culminating in truth.

have first of their causes or generation." The key word is ratiocination, that is to say, conceptual reasoning applied to the causes of appearances. What matters, therefore, for Hobbes is the rational causality of appearances, which involve three notions, motion, space and body. Descartes' rationalism, far from accepting these three notions as basic, was led to believe that they might all be illusions, and that the only thing that matters, as proof of existence, is the thinking subject. Yet in the end, since space in Hobbesian thought has no other reality except that of the thinking mind, we are led to a similar subjectivism, which, as with Descartes, opens the way to immanentism and to relativism in ethics. "Whatever is the object of any man's appetite or desire," says Hobbes, "that is it which he for his part calleth Good: and the object of his hate and aversion, Evil. . . . For these words of Good and Evil . . . are ever used with relation to the person that useth them. There being nothing simply and absolutely so; nor any common rule of Good and Evil to be taken from the nature of the objects themselves."* Besides this relativism in ethics, he rejoins both Descartes and Pascal in his distrust of imagination or fancy, and in looking upon poetry as mere adornment, as secondary to judgement as experience is to reason. With such views, which were part of English and French thought, it is easy to understand how and why, both in France and in England, poetry moved towards conceptualism, that is to say in fact, towards the implementation of Boileau's dictum, *"Ce que l'on conçoit bien s'énonce clairement"*, and towards the notion that poetic diction and fancy are merely used as additives to render judgement and order palatable. Hobbes' attitude towards imagination and poetry, shared by Locke in England and Descartes and Pascal in France, underlies the changes in poetry which took place in these countries during the Classical age and the age of reason. Hobbes' rationalism reduces the world to what reason can apprehend and understand, and for him true knowledge could only come from reason. Sense or perceptual knowledge was therefore not considered as true knowledge, and so Hobbes' philosophy oscillates between materialism and subjectivism, and will, as far as the subjectivist aspect of it is concerned, culminate, like Cartesian philosophy, in Hegelianism.

* *Leviathan* (O.U.P.), p. 41.

Locke was neither a mathematician nor a subjective rationalist; he was above all an experimentalist and a humanist. He did not believe in the possible dissolution of substance into extension and in the omnipotence of reason; he believed reason to be limited and only able to pierce a part of the mystery of creation. Thence his complete lack of arrogance, his natural humility and tolerance for other people's views. "We stand," he said, "outside the things of this world, and our ideas of them leave us in ignorance of their essence, and if we do not understand the finite things of the world, how much more shall we not understand ourselves, and the still higher spiritual beings which God has created, and above all God Himself." This admirable statement about the limits of human understanding, central to his philosophy, is also basic to the English ethos; it explains a great deal of the English lack of mental arrogance and, more significantly, their fundamental political and religious tolerance. With Locke, God is neither snuffed out of existence, as with Descartes, nor dissolved into the burning light of man's mind, as with Hobbes. He is, on the contrary, accepted as the centre of creation, knowledge of whom can only be obtained through revelation or through the mediation of God's angels and higher spirits. In contradistinction with Pascal, who believed that reason could only lead to the threshold of the choice or leap into faith, Locke was convinced of the rationality of the existence of God: "It is plain to me, we have a more certain knowledge of the existence of a God than of anything our senses have not immediately discovered to us." Being on the threshold of the age of reason, an age which rejected religion, it is important to remember that Locke, whose importance as the expression of the sensibility of the people to whom he belonged cannot be overrated, was not only a rationalist empiricist, but also a true Christian thinker whose tolerant, rational Christianity connects him directly with Erasmus. Faith for him could not be divorced from reason, and his essay *The Reasonableness of Christianity as Delivered in the Scriptures* justifies this attitude, and his belief that "faith is nothing else but an assent founded on the highest reason" was echoed two centuries and a half later by the words of another great Englishman, Cardinal Newman, who said: "Christian faith is the perfection of human intelligence." Pascal's distinction between reasons of the heart and reason is very close to Locke's distinction between "sensitive knowledge of the existence of things, demonstrative knowledge of the existence of God, and assent to Christian revelation". This assent is, in fact, very close to the leap into faith of Pascal. Whether Locke, who spent many years in Holland and France, had read or not the *Pensées*, which came out in 1670, also the year of the publication of Spinoza's *Ethics*, or Mme. Perrier's life of Pascal, which came out in 1684, is irrelevant; the fact is that these two very devout Christian thinkers had very many ideas and beliefs in common. For both of them the most important fact was that man, *"ce roseau pensant"*, caught between two infinites, plagued by the limitation of his reason, could best do justice to his noble and tragic humanity by accepting his limitations and, therefore, by being most divine when he was most humble and tolerant of the unavoidable human mediocrities, failings and weaknesses. Reason, the essence of man, one of his essential connections with God, must not be, as it was going to be later, deified, for, by being so, it does not elevate man, it destroys him. The closeness between aspects of Locke's and Pascal's thought, echoing in many ways the closeness between Hobbes' and Descartes' thought, shows that, with certain differences of emphasis and a certain time-lag in the development of the sensibility of the two countries, the spiritual climates of Britain and France were never very far apart.

Such was not quite the case with painting, for if Le Nain and Latour have affinities with their great contemporaries—Rembrandt, Vermeer, Peter de Hooch and Velasquez—Poussin is, on the contrary, an integral part of French classicism, whose place is side by side with Racine. Like him, he has fully assimilated his sustained studies of antique models, and, like him, he has been able to blend into a whole the classical purity of forms and the psychological insight which are the hallmarks of seventeenth-century French art. Yet the landscape paintings at the end of his life, and particularly the admirable landscape paintings of Claude Le Lorrain, indicate a reverence for the majesty, mysteries and beauty of nature, shorn of any pantheistic suggestions within perfectly controlled forms, which opened up a new approach to Nature as an intrinsic source of artistic creativity. From Racine to La Rochefoucauld, La Bruyère, Fénelon, St. Evremond, Bayle and Descartes himself, the study of the human psyche was one of the main preoccupations of French artists and thinkers of that time. This search went on side by side with the utmost control of expression and purity of form. The heart could very well be torn to shreds, as is so often the case in Racine, yet the expression of such a state was submitted to the most rigorous control. The molten lava of passions was always compelled to flow through rigorous, beautifully shaped moulds, and, whatever happened behind them, the great façades of the Louvre, the impassive, austere colonnades of Versailles, only spoke of order, tranquillity and undisturbed hierarchy. With them, there were none of the joyful frolics and gay abandon of Italian or German Baroque art. On the other hand, English art neither indulged the *rococo* of Italy nor the monumental austerity of French art. It had, as usual, its own flavour: a combination of decorum, majesty and naturalness, of which Wren's St. Paul's is the best example. This naturalness was a great attraction for many Frenchmen who visited London at that time or who, like St. Evremond, found there their spiritual home. He prepared the way for Montesquieu and Voltaire, and at that time the exchanges between England and France were wide-ranging and numerous in all domains, including the throne, with Henrietta Maria as wife of Charles I.

VIII

Eighteenth Century

The eighteenth century, the age of Enlightenment, the age of reason, the century of light, or *Le Grand Siècle* as Michelet put it, does not of course begin in 1700 and end in 1800, though it can be safely said that the sensibility which marks approximately the first two-thirds of this century, a period described in England as the Augustan Age, extends in France from the death of Louis XIV to the premonitory tremors of the Revolution. Both English and French society are, at that moment, at very similar levels of development. They both tend towards greater and greater urbanization, increasing well-being in the middle and upper middle classes, and commercial expansion in far-flung parts of the globe, until the conflicts for the snatching of these various colonial possessions begin in the second half of the century. In both cases, a great deal of the life of the two countries is centred on the life of their capitals, London and Paris. London, following the great fire of 1666, which gave Christopher Wren the chance of rebuilding St. Paul's, had been transformed into a modern city. The wealth and power of Louis XIV, the administrative ability of Louvois and Colbert, the vital importance of life at court, that is to say, in Paris, all contributed to the growing importance and architectural beauty of that city. The capital cities of both England and France have played a vital part in the arts of their people. From Villon to Baudelaire and Léon-Paul Fargues, from Defoe to Dickens and T. S. Eliot, Paris and London have been the inspiration of much poetry. At that time, the arts and literature were therefore the product of urbanized societies dominated by the notion of the 'gentleman' on one side of the Channel and *l'honnête homme* on the other. Manners, courtliness, control, were the ethical criteria of people who moved about more in coaches than on their feet, and who looked at nature more through the windows of their houses and carriages than with their naked eyes. Such, of course, was not the case for the bulk of the people, hard at work in order to earn their livelihood, but these people were neither the concern of art nor themselves interested in it.

But England and France, though socially similar in many respects, were quite different on the political plane. In the middle of the seventeenth century, the English had had their revolution which, in spite of all the Hobbesian respect for authority, had led to the beheading of the King. This had shattered Europe and shown that, when it came to political freedom, the English did not flinch from the harshest measures. The French, as deeply attracted to freedom as the English, were deeply impressed. The lesson soaked in, and in due course, in their turn, they made use of it with a vengeance. English poets were as enthusiastic about the French Revolution as French philosophers like Montesquieu and Voltaire had been enthusiastic about England's political liberalism and philosophical greatness. Voltaire sang Newton's glory in numbers:

> "*Confidents du Très-Haut, substances éternelles,*
> *Qui brûlez de ses feux, qui couvrez de vos ailes*
> *Le trône où votre maître est assis parmi vous,*
> *Parlez: du grand Newton n'étiez-vous point jaloux?*"

Pope had anticipated him with the words:

> "Nature and Nature's laws lay hid in night,
> God said let Newton be and all was light."

After the death of Louis XIV, the authoritarian structure, which had been imposed upon politics and society, began to weigh heavily upon the classes which bore the brunt of endless wars and the burdens of all sorts of exactions and taxes. They longingly turned their gaze towards England, as the land of freedom which had already established a political system based on respect for the law. France had to wait one hundred and fifty years before she could attempt to implement ideals, which, if applied fully, would turn the earth into a kind of Heaven. During the eighteenth century, England and France, while their colonial rivalries had not yet come to a head, were full of mutual admiration, and the names of Newton and Locke rang throughout Europe, which reached perhaps then the zenith of cosmopolitanism. Voltaire travelled all over

Europe, including Russia where he was listened to with reverence, and Mozart was as much acclaimed in Paris as Haydn was in London. If there is a philosophy which truly expresses English liberalism and political maturity, it is the philosophy of Locke. His lack of dogmatism, his assertion that all knowledge is derived from experience, something which links him with Ockham, his belief that even revelation must be judged by reason, his theory of the separation of the executive from the legislative power, something which France has only fully achieved in the last twelve years, gave him an enormous influence in a country which was still in the throes of autocracy and intolerance. Locke's rational empiricism, reinforced by Hume's and Berkeley's, and partly accepted by Kant, who tried to bridge the gap between metaphysical and practical reason, has been one of the two strong currents of western thought. He even formulated, before Karl Marx, the theory, the origin of which goes back to Aquinas, that the value of any given product should be based on the work involved. The influence of Locke in Europe was much enhanced by the acknowledged greatness of Newton, and Voltaire's *Lettres sur les Anglais* and his *Eléments de la philosophie de Newton*, have done more than anything to spread this influence. Rousseau, who made a brief visit to England and who had such a great influence on the French Revolution and on Romanticism, was deeply impressed by Locke's political and educational theories.

Even though Locke was religious, he too had ended in accepting the separation between rational knowledge and assent to religious experience, something which, in the end, converges towards the separation between transcendence and immanence, which naturally flows from Descartes' philosophy, strengthened by Hobbes' immanentist and materialist thought. The end of the seventeenth century marks, in fact, the end of metaphysics and of a unified vision of the world. Transcendence becomes fully separated from immanence. God, Descartes' prime mover, has faded into Limbo, and His creation, man, has acquired immanence and can emulate Him through his capacity to think and to feel. Yet, as these two aspects of the human person, which are reason, meaning, in fact, understanding working through concepts and perceptions based on sense-data, and feelings which are mostly confined to sensations and to the reactions of the heart, are kept apart, the separation between reason and feelings widens, and while the century wears on, we have a growing shift from the Cartesian "I think therefore I am" to the "I feel therefore I am". Feelings unprocessed by or no longer sifted through reason, as was the case when transcendence and immanence were connected, and when man was an integral part of creation, soon turn into sentimentality. Enthusiasm, which at the beginning of the century had been frowned upon and kept in check, soon overflows in various forms, such as Methodism in England and the works of Rousseau in France, and in both cases it ended in assuming an enormous influence in the life of these two countries. Methodism had played an important part politically in the life of this country and in that of the U.S.A., and it has resulted in the fact that English socialism has been firmly grounded on religious thought. As men are generally moved more by passions and emotions than by reason, the Great Revolution, as far as ideas are concerned, owes far more to Rousseau than to Voltaire, the Encyclopedists, or any other protagonists of thought. The Encyclopedists and Voltaire wanted reform; Rousseau wanted change, and the economic conditions required it. This was, in fact, the perfect Marxist formula for revolution.

Religion, which can no longer stand the test of reason, turns to piety, enthusiasm and various aspects of spiritualism. Voltaire's battle-cry *Ecrasons l'infâme* suits a society, which, intent upon sensations, looks upon art not as a search for or revelation of truth, but as the refined and crowning accomplishment of an extremely civilized society, and as a means to satisfy its longing for dreams and for sensations. The importance of sensations necessarily implies the importance of the present, of the moment when the sensation is experienced and which is equated with the awareness of existence itself. Thence, of course, the urge to continuously grasp sensations and the ever renewed sour taste left behind by their disappearance, so admirably conveyed by the paintings of Watteau, in front of which one can feel that a sensation is no sooner felt than it has disappeared, and that one has to search over and over again for new sensations in order to feel alive. This desperate quest for sensations, through love, music or *fêtes*, is shot through with melancholy and with the unavoidable sense of decay and destruction which lurks in every rose. Watteau's grace, transparency of colours and overhanging drama, are pure music orchestrated in colours and volumes. Watteau's *fêtes* and *voyages* call for the music of Mozart, who, if he was not quite his contemporary, was a man of the same historical period and who, strangely enough, had practically as short a life. The name of Mozart summons that of Haydn, and particularly that of Johann Sebastian Bach, the greatest religious composer, not to say, as some would have it, the greatest composer, who ever lived. What matters, in this context, is that Bach testifies to the fact that, in spite of Hobbes, Voltaire and others, religion was anything but dead; in fact, it continued to inspire great art, great architecture, great painting and great music. Baroque art was then at its zenith, and churches and opera houses were competing in profane elegance and decorations and, all in all, although Beethoven composed his greatest masterpieces in the Romantic age, it is reasonable to concede to the eighteenth century the honour of being the golden age of music.

The Augustan age is the Classical age of England, in the sense that the ideas which dominated French classicism are then admired and, to a certain extent, applied in English literature, and, what is more, applied by writers of genius like Pope and Dryden. The similarities between Pope and Boileau, and between Dryden and Racine, do not need to be laboured. With these writers, the alexandrine and the couplet are fully adopted in English literature by great poets. Molière's influence in England is widely recognized, and there is no doubt that in the Augustan age Racinian tragedy is more alive on this side of the Channel than in the hands of De la Motte, Crébillon, or Voltaire, who only caught the Racinian appearance without the substance. At first glance, the emperor looks fully clad, but one soon realizes that this is merely a dummy and that there is no living emperor under the clothes. The same criticism of shallowness can be levelled at Diderot's melodramas. In fact, the age of reason singularly lacks imagination, and without imagination there is no poetry. The verses of Voltaire have little to do with poetry, neither have those of Jean Baptiste Rousseau, Le Franc de Pompignan or Piron. Something similar to what happened in France happened in England after Pope and Dryden. Just as Voltaire failed to realize that the climate for Racinian tragedy was no longer there, and that one cannot create tragedy by merely producing the appearance of it, in the same way the poets of minor gifts, who immediately followed Dryden and Pope, failed to notice or to feel the change in sensibility and, consequently, the need for new forms. Like Voltaire in France, they confined themselves to producing the appearance without the substance. In fact, just as Voltaire, although he was a genius, was a very second-rate poet, and certainly no genius in poetry, in the same way some of the immediate followers of Pope and Dryden were endowed with only minor talent, and the proof that they were so lies primarily not in their very minor productions, but in the fact that, lacking genius, they could not apprehend and express the new sensibility which required new forms. They merely produced not creative, revelatory poetry, but what Hopkins aptly described as "Parnassian poetry", that is to say, poetry which merely repeats old, existing forms without any revelation of new truths. The poets who, like Cowper, Thomson, Young and Gray, were better equipped and, consequently, were vaguely aware of the new sensibility, the sensibility which was soon to find expression in Burns, Blake and the Romantics, produced poetry which, though minor, is poetry and not merely verse, as was the case in France between Racine and André Chénier. Besides that, barely a generation, which was in fact anything but barren of poetry, separates Pope and Dryden from Burns and Blake, while at least three generations lie between the death of Racine and the birth of André Chénier and the emergence of the new sensibility with Rousseau.

Round about that time, that is to say, round about the middle of the century, both countries show a more and more marked separation between intellect and feelings which turned to sentiments. Richardson, Sterne, l'Abbé Prévost, melodrama on both sides of the Channel, the attraction of rusticity and pastoral verse, clearly indicate a growing interest in nature, the great divinity of the Romantic age, and marked changes in sensibility. Until then, nature has been essentially unnatural. Both English and French painters were, above all, society painters, and their periwigged, powdered ladies and gentlemen were so swaddled in clothes that one could hardly discern the human shape hidden under them. Whenever the women were shorn of their protective garments, they were painted as Rubensian Venuses sporting themselves all too obviously in order to attract the male, whose main preoccupation was, like that of his partner, to cultivate sensations. Boucher, Fragonard and Watteau are, if not brothers, certainly cousins of Reynolds, Romney and Gainsborough.

But this, of course, is anything but the whole picture. The courtly ladies of the eighteenth century were not all engrossed in kindling men's concupiscence or in pursuing purely material and fleeting pleasures; many of them were also the inspirers and the guides of a good deal that was noble and elevating in French life; they were more than anybody else responsible for making of Paris the great intellectual centre of the time. Besides, if Fragonard and Boucher lack depth, the same cannot be said of Watteau, whose *Embarquement pour Cythère* and *Gilles the Clown* exhibit truly tragic intensity. A contemporary of Watteau, Nordlain de la Gourdaune, painted an imitation of *l'Embarquement pour Cythère*, and gave it a fluidity of colouring which already suggests Turner and a new approach to paintings. Chardin, the greatest painter of the age, shows that all the energy and vitality of France were not concentrated in urbanized life and in intellectual pursuits and refined quests for sensations. Continuing the tradition of Le Nain, Teniers and Flemish and Dutch painters, he has endowed certain aspects of the life of the middle class and the working class with the kind of noble simplicity and profundity which transcends time. The objects of his paintings are alive, and they are an integral part of organic relationships which form wholes in which mind and emotions are not separated.

If England's courtly painters join hands with Boucher and Fragonard, the Scots painters Raeburn and Ramsay join hands with Chardin, not because they painted similar subjects, since they were essentially portrait painters, but because they exhibit the same realism, which is also the hallmark of Scottish art throughout the ages. Raeburn's *Mrs. Scott-Moncrieff*, Alan Ramsay's *Rousseau*, are inspired, direct expositions of the sitters' personalities, untramelled by concepts. The masterly handling of colours in *Mrs. Scott-Moncrieff* exudes intellect and sensuousness, and the mysterious shades and moist gaze in *Rousseau* glisten with reflections of new worlds. At the same time as Ramsay, Raeburn and David Hume, there lived in Edinburgh, to say nothing of glorious yet cantankerous visitors like Rousseau or sin-obsessed Boswell, the brothers Adam, who were transforming Edinburgh and launching a new style of architecture in Europe. At about the same time was born Robert Burns, who exemplifies better than any Scot the blend between realism and sentiment, and between intellectual rigour and passionate belief, which characterizes the Scots genius.

French and English eighteenth-century rationalisms certainly have a great deal in common, but they also have marked differences. They have in common a distrust of dogmatism, a love for tolerance and a definite zeal for humanistic and social improvements. The differences are important. There is indeed quite a distance between Humean scepticism, which fuses the in-se of reality with the consciousness of the perception of this reality, something which in fact rejoins Berkeleyan idealism, and the reformatory zeal and concern for reality of the French *philosophes*. It is in fact the difference between thought abstracted from reality, being the basis of reality, and thought in action. Hume and Berkeley are more direct heirs of Descartes than Voltaire and Diderot. With them, English empiricism has been subsumed, and for that one might blame the non-Englishness of Hume and Berkeley, into a form of idealism which leaves reality untouched, reduces it to the consciousness of its perception and, in the case of Berkeley, bases the very existence of reality on the consciousness of the thinking subject. I could not better outline these differences than by allowing Hegel to give his views on the subject. This is what he says:

"What is admirable and what underlies the importance of French philosophical writings is their astonishing energy—that is to say, the strength of thought struggling against existence, against faith, against the power of a thousand years of established authority. What is admirable is the basic characteristic which is the most profound feeling of indignation against the acceptance of anything alien to the consciousness of self, against what tries to be without it, or in places where it cannot be. . . . French atheism, materialism and naturalism, are associated with a profound feeling of indignation against uncritical presuppositions and the positive values of religion, right, morality and civic institutions. They oppose them from a ground of common sense and seriousness, and on account of their desire to conceive of the absolute as being present both as thought and as absolute unity. . . . In order to build their political constitution, the French have started from the abstract and universal thoughts which are the negative elements of reality. In order to build theirs, the English have started from concrete reality in order to make of it an homogeneous whole. Their writers have not risen to universal principles. . . . The French have established general definitions and thoughts, and have stood by them. . . . Cartesian philosophy was only abstract metaphysics; now we have principles based on the concrete. . . . The French, with their universal mind, have fought with wit against the speculative concept, while the Germans have done so with common sense. We find in the French a profound philosophic need which embraces all things; in contradistinction with the English, the Scots and even the Germans, they are full of life. They have a universal and concrete view of the whole, which is independent of authority or of any abstract metaphysics. Their method always consists in a development from perceptions and sensations; it is a grandiose concept which never loses sight of the whole. . . . French philosophers show above all indignation against immorality; their attacks, sometimes full of common sense, sometimes full of wit and sometimes full of good arguments, are never directed against what we call religion. . . . It is easy to reproach the French with their attacks against religion and against the state. In order to fully assess the merits of these writers, one must bear in mind the dreadful conditions of the society they were living in and the misery and turpitude which prevailed at that moment in France. . . . These writers were supposed to attack religion, the state and morality. But which religion are they talking about? They are talking about a religion which was the most stupid set of superstitions, bad priesthood, obtuseness, debauchery and corruption of temporal goods in the middle of public wretchedness. As for the state, what kind of state was it? It was a state marked by the ruthless domination of ministers, their whores, their chambermaids and valets, a host of lazy petty tyrants who felt that they had a divine right to pillage the wealth of the state and to use the sweat of the people."*

* Hegel, *Lectures on the History of Philosophy*, vol. III, pp. 506–518, translated from the first edition of the *Complete Works*.

IX

Romantic Age

Well before the birth of Burns and Blake, in 1754, Rousseau had already published his famous discourse *Sur l'origine et le fondement de l'inégalité parmi les hommes*, and Romanticism had already begun. If one chooses to describe Rousseau or Chateaubriand as the forerunners of Romanticism, then the question is, how should one describe Richardson, Collins, Thomson, Gray, l'Abbé Prévost, Young and others? For, after all, with them, *le mal du siècle* had already begun. Besides these names, it is not difficult to quote other names which would show that some of the traits which are part and parcel of Romanticism, particularly the love of nature, have, in varying degrees, been present in the works of many writers or artists throughout the centuries. Naturally the love of nature of Du Bellay, St. Amant, Claude Le Lorrain or La Fontaine, is not a Wordsworthian or Coleridgean love of nature, yet it certainly was one aspect of it, and the difference between the two is only a matter of degree, based primarily on the attitude to religion. It is, indeed, the difference between the concept of Nature as part of God's creation, yet separated from Him, and that of Nature as informed with and suffused into the Divine. In spite of Spinoza, pantheism only reached its climax in the second half of the eighteenth century. The Coleridgean *Apostrophe to Nature*,

> "O dread and silent mount! I gazed upon thee
> Till thou, still present to the bodily senses,
> Didst vanish from my thought; entranced in prayer
> I worshipped the invisible alone",

could not have been uttered by La Fontaine, who lived in a world in which subject and object were separated, even though both were still parts of a metaphysical universe. But Coleridge's utterance could have been, and was, repeated by Rousseau, Wordsworth, Thoreau, Constable, and by practically every notable writer or artist of the Romantic age. It indicates a new approach to Nature, that is to say, a new sensibility, which had been groping towards self-consciousness and which, in France, fully emerged into consciousness through the genius of Rousseau.

By bringing out into men's consciousness the vast upsurge of feelings which view man as naturally good yet corrupted by society, and nature as the great mother, source of noble and human inspirations, Rousseau is by far the greatest influence of the second half of the eighteenth century and, all in all, since his influence is not without effect even today, probably the greatest literary influence of modern times. It was his belief that men ought to be free and equal, something which, more than anything else, informed the American and the French revolutions. It is with Rousseau that the man of feelings emerges in full daylight, and it is he who, more aptly than anyone else, echoed Descartes' words "I think therefore I am" with the far more potent words "I feel therefore I am". Nature with Rousseau, Wordsworth and the great Romantic writers is ethical. It commands certain definite attitudes towards men and the universe; it cannot condone falseness, inequalities or tyrannies in human kind. All the great English poets of the Romantic age hailed the French Revolution as the dawn of a new age, and before them, Burns and Blake, both deeply disturbed by what they saw around them, had raised great protests in the name of the dual belief that "A man's a man for a' that" and "All men shall brothers be". All the preachings of sweet reason could not allay the qualms of the heart of the artists or of the men of vision, for it is all too easy to say that man is a rational animal, or to preach tolerance to those who have nothing to endure except the outrages of excessive well-being. Perhaps eighteenth century reason was, as A. N. Whitehead put it, only "one-eyed reason". Whatever it was, the fact is that all its comforting music could not drown Rousseau's stern cry, "Man is born free, and everywhere he is in chains". This cry was soon to echo throughout Europe, and at its sound many chains were to fall, to be, alas, all too soon replaced by other chains.

At the heart of the rising industrial prosperity of the age, the cleavage between a society more and more engrossed in material values and the artist's search for naked truth was already such that Blake, the first of *les poètes maudits*, was looked upon as mad, simply because he could see with his naked eye visions of true essence and the future Jerusalem in broad daylight, while most of his fellow beings could only see growing profits and material comforts, amidst underfed, oppressed slave-labour. In this house that Reason had built, Blake could see the irrational and anti-divine, ruthlessly crushing the hearts of men in the name of pseudo-religion and social conventions. So he was driven to conclude that the heart must leap beyond reason, and that the "tyger burning bright In the forest of the night" is the obsessive glimmer which haunts the darkness surrounding every God-orientated human being, who is intent upon grasping the true mystery of life and upon meeting God at last face to face. The final answer to this question no man can give. Rembrandt offered his own answer with *The Three Crosses* and the *Supper at Emmaus*. Blake gave his own in his *Songs of Innocence and Experience*, which are not, of course, a definitive answer, but which, by being flashes of light, illuminations in the human night, assert the triumph of man over his fate and over the mystery which surrounds him. Burns, if he did not quite possess Blake's imagination, had a similar vision of innocence, of beauty and of the lyricism of life, so often destroyed by humbug and by conventions disguised as religious faith and morality. In France, in book after book, tossed up here and there in the course of his wandering life, Rousseau was steadily feeding the flood-tides which soon were to burst and sweep away the rotten social edifice, so as to replace it by the perfect geometry of the *contrat social* and the supremacy of humanized reason.

By the end of this century, when the tide of protest and reform reached its peak, the old edifice was duly swept away and a new age was begun, with even a new calendar, carrying with it a flurry of neo-classicism, which brought France back to Graeco-Roman days with consuls, emperors, peplums, chlamydes and Graecian hairstyles. The world was new again, but it did not last; it could not last. All round France environing monarchs were anxious about their tottering thrones, and their aristocratic, bourgeois or trading subjects were all anxious about their wealth. In France, most members of these classes reconciled themselves to their losses, while many of them took the royal road to Cologne and London, in order to prepare the bandwaggon of the *émigrés*, in which they would return to France and kick into their places the *va-nu-pieds* of the Revolution. They did not have to wait long; everything conspired to help them, particularly ambition at all levels, from honour-surfeited generals and wealth-bloated ministers, and within two generations France was practically back to where it had started, with the middle class fully in the saddle and the old soured *grognards* dreaming in dereliction and penury of the meteor which, for twenty years, they had followed throughout Europe. Yet if the surface of things seemed more or less unaltered, the undercurrent was different. The great wave which had surged from the depth of time and which, fed by all the sorrows, frustrations and sufferings of centuries of oppression, had overthrown the régime in France, never again returned to quietude. Its pent-up, frustrated fury constantly made its presence felt throughout the nineteenth century, and at the beginning of the twentieth, and it exploded again on different shores and under different skies with even greater violence than before, and yet with results similar to those of 1789, which were, and are, that those who sweat and bleed to plough the earth and plant new crops are never, alas, those who reap the fruits of the new growths. A new authority, wearing new clothes, claiming new ideals, clamps again the same iron yoke of domination on the remainder of the revolutionaries or on their sons, and continues to exploit them practically as they were exploited before. It will no doubt be so over and over again, and one wonders how often their cataclysmic upsurges will have to be repeated before men accept, at last, Rousseau's Messianic belief that men were born free and that they must live in freedom and not in chains, whether the chains be political, economic or religious. Such is the law of Nature, for Nature is only 'red in tooth and claw' because men made it so in their own image, in order to excuse their own brutality and acquisitiveness. But Nature is neither gratuitously brutal nor, least of all, acquisitive; it is organized and integrated according to its own rules of development and growth. Although as a vast gestating womb, continuously transforming and creating life, it carries with it the immutable process of one thing feeding upon another, as man himself does, there are no examples in Nature of sweated labour or, for instance, of exploitations of herds of antelopes ploughing fields to grow grass to feed other antelopes, or other animals which use them as means to assert their own power and importance or to impress other animals. If tigers feed on lambs or other animals, they do so as part of the same necessity which compels man to do likewise, including those who are vegetarians, for vegetables also have life, to say nothing of fish, but they do not do so in order to build palaces or to go for holidays in the Bahamas at the expense of sweated labour in some satanic mills.

Wordsworth, Coleridge, Constable, Turner, Keats, Shelley, all of them felt strongly about the unnatural exploitation of men by men and, like Rousseau, equated love of nature with love of man, simplicity and lack of pomp and conventions. A cabin in a wood, as with Thoreau, a cottage in the Lake District, as with Wordsworth, a little house on an island, as with Rousseau, a country or a sea shore maisonette, as with Constable or Turner, those were the places where the true life could be lived, and not in the salons or mansions of London or Paris. Religion was dead, killed by Reason, which was deified by the French Revolution. But the attempt to deify Reason was condemned to failure, for man cannot worship abstractions, and that is why the new religion propounded by Rousseau and the great Romantics had a better chance of success. Nature and its various manifestations, trees, forests, mountains, seas and lakes, have majesty, grandeur, sublimity and a kind of religious aura about them. A forest is a church, a mountain is a divinity, and the many voiced sea can whisper of Eternity. This love of Nature could not but strike a strongly hierarchised, soulless society as very unnatural, and that is why the Romantics, poets and artists, fled from this uncongenial society, either into Nature, into the past among the ruins of a lost golden age in exotic lands of dreams and imaginations, or into the world of legends and myths of other cultures. The present for them is no longer a moment of plenitude, as in pure eighteenth-century sensualism; it is, on the contrary, a moment of anxiety and frustration.

Promethean man, rational man, has stolen fire from heaven, but this fire gives neither comfort nor heat; it merely illumines the picture of the lost Eden, and this picture eats out his heart and causes him more suffering than the vultures on the Caucasian Rock. Peace only lies in Nature and in imagination, and all the

Romantic poets have relied on memory and imagination as the means to apprehend the real and to transcend time. No one relied more on imagination than Napoleon, according to Hegel the *zeitgeist* of the age, praised by Byron, Shelley, Goethe and Beethoven, who admittedly scored off the dedication to the Third Symphony but left untouched the record of the imaginative encounter of his musical genius with the genius of war and politics, who, from the Pyramids to Moscow never forgot to carry with him his copy of Ossian's poems, a work of pure imagination if ever there is one. Napoleon, the most extraordinary blend of imagination and positivistic rationalism, dreaming of Caesar and Alexander, Hegelian-born before Hegel, sought before him to turn the imaginary and the material world into the new reality. He did not succeed, but he left the world dazzled by his rise and fall, and he gave a new dimension to Milton's Lucifer, which that great Scots poet, Byron, paraded about under the name of Satan. In spite of their greatness, it was not Wordsworth, Coleridge or Shelley who evoked interest and wide recognition in Europe, but Byron; it was he, admired by all, from poets like Goethe to Princes and Countesses, who, like his great hero, had the inspired sense of going to die on a rocky island, not of war wounds but of illness. He did not have a suitable gaoler to burnish his martyr's statue, like Mary Stuart or Napoleon, but he had his defeated hopes which, together with the glory that was Greece oppressed by the Turks, supplied and continue to supply a brilliant halo to his immortality. No French poet could hold a candle, in the realms of publicity, to Byron's life and death, not even Victor Hugo pacing up and down through the mist in the island of Jersey.

French, English and Scottish poets, Romantics all, were nevertheless quite different. The time-lag, which had brought a strong flavour of French classicism to England in its Augustan age, had again set in, and with the great exception of Rousseau, it can be said that English Romanticism was ahead, by at least a season, of French Romanticism, which only caught up with it with symbolist poetry. The same phenomenon, which had time and time again taken place, took place once more. Sensibility had changed, but French poets, lacking genius, had kept to the old forms, the old rhetoric, the old neo-classicism which easily confused eloquence with poetry, a confusion which went on until the second half of the nineteenth century, when it ended with the visionary poetry of Hugo and with the Symbolists. French Romantic poets took only the husk of things, while they remained unaware of the core; they concentrated on external modifications, on techniques, and not on the creativeness of form, and, in spite of their claims of revolutionary changes, they made no profound changes in poetry. The poetic experience is still organized or recounted logically according to the rules of rhetoric, and not according to developing affective patterns which the poet discovers and suggests in a way which is also a source of creativeness for the reader. The rhetoric of Victor Hugo is different from that of Corneille, but it is still rhetoric; it is more emotional, more colourful, more laden with perceptual data, but it is still as dialectical; it aims at convincing the heart more than the mind, but conviction remains, nevertheless, the aim. Like Voltaire, he is concerned with expressing his "philosophy", and although Voltaire's cerebrations are certainly different from his emotional rhetoric, we have in both cases, rhetoric, which, of course, with Victor Hugo can rise to great poetry. One might be thoroughly repelled by the lapses into vulgarity, the bad taste, pose, humourlessness, Gongorism, sentimentality and conceptualism which mar so much of Victor Hugo's work, but one cannot deny that he is a great poet. His claims,

> *"Je fis souffler un vent révolutionnaire,*
> *Je mis un bonnet rouge au vieux dictionnaire"*

are, like Gautier's gaudy waistcoat, part of the means *pour épater le bourgeois*, and Flaubert, for whom the only Romantic was Michelet, aptly describes Hugo as *"un classique révolutionnaire"*.

By the time Romantic exuberance and exhibitionism had turned to sour fruit and sere leaves, science, the last born of *la pensée* so highly praised by Vigny, was on the ascendancy; realism, control, plasticity were the new watchwords for jaded sensibilities that wanted a rest from the ceaseless tides of sentiments: *"Je hais le mouvement qui déplace les lignes"*, said Baudelaire; and the Parnassians echoed his views in lapidary poetry. Leconte de Lisle, haunted by a nostalgia for the exotic landscapes amidst which he had been born, revels in violent contrasts of colours set still and motionless on the canvas of his poems, which are, like Gauguin's

Tahitian pictures, a strange harmony of dissonances. The music of this new verse is syncopated, jerky and fit for a kind of primitive dance with jingling bells, tambourines, and bejewelled arms and ankles glittering in the dazzling sun. The listener or onlooker, stunned and entranced, watches breathlessly this primeval violence of nature and its inhabitants, "red in tooth and claw", giving a demonstration of Darwinism:

"Midi, roi des étés, épandu sur la plaine,
Tombe en nappes d'argent des hauteurs du ciel bleu".

The earth stifles, elephants trample across red sands, lions sleep, while condors soar high over the snowy peaks of the Andes. Gautier, whom Baudelaire over-generously described as *"le parfait magician ès lettres françaises"*, Banville, Hérédia, Sully Prudhomme and many other poets, known as the *Parnasse*, concentrated on plasticity—arrested imagery, jewel words or lines—and produced one or two memorable examples of minor writing; but their flight from the restlessness and proneness to emotionalism of the Romantics towards sculptural beauty and stony heart does not indicate any change in sensibility, which is the only true sign of the renewal of poetry and art. With them, it was still fragmented art, creation without a prime mover, and still the same flight away from the present into antiquity or exotic landscapes. No attempts were made towards integration or towards facing the problems of modern life.

These were the achievements of Nerval and the Symbolists. Symbolism as a literary movement is difficult to characterize in a few words; it includes a new and widely shared form of sensibility and a new approach to poetry. All one can do is to try to sum up, as briefly as possible, the main traits which mark the individuality of some of the principal representatives of that movement. Nerval is generally not included in it, yet his strange genius, markedly attuned to the Germans Novalis and Hölderlin and to the English poets Coleridge and Shelley, is the first in France to exteriorize clearly an awareness of the mysterious life of nature and of the complex interpenetration of man's thoughts and feelings and perceptions. It is he who, much more than Baudelaire, sought *"l'épanchement du rêve dans la vie réelle"*, and who said:

Britain and France, The Unruly Twins

"A la matière même un verbe est attaché
Un pur esprit s'accroît sous l'écorce des pierres".

One looks in vain in French Romantic poetry for the kind of close union between man and nature which pervades the poetry of Wordsworth, Coleridge and Shelley. Lamartine wonders and questions: *"Objets inanimés, avez-vous donc une âme?"*; for Vigny nature is indifferent, and for Musset and the early Hugo she is part of the properties of poetry, but she is never a "symbolic image of the mind", as Novalis defined her; she is not the mysterious echo of a world beyond the senses, which the poet, through the magic of his words and through the permanence of myths and perennial symbols, seeks to bring to life. It is Gérard de Nerval, whose disequilibrated genius could not resist in the end the pressure of mystery which it could apprehend, who heralds the true changes in sensibility which Baudelaire in his best moments was going to exteriorize, when, as Rimbaud said, he became *voyant* and had access to *le monde du rêve*.

"Baudelaire," says T. S. Eliot,[*] "is indeed the greatest exemplar in modern poetry in any language, for his verse and language is the nearest thing to a complete renovation that we have experienced." This opinion, which Valéry later echoed with the words *"Baudelaire est au comble de la gloire"*, is widely accepted, and it recognizes in Baudelaire a great poet and the most important poetic landmark of the last hundred years. But if Baudelaire can rightly be considered the best representative of the new sensibility, it does not mean that he created it. His famous sonnet, *Correspondences*, has too often been described as one of the twelve slabs which the new Moses of art brought back from Mount Sinai and gave as law to his fellow artists. It is nothing of the kind. The belief in the correspondence between the world of the senses and the mysterious reality which could be the ideal world of Plato, is barely hinted at, though of course there is plenty of evidence in Baudelaire's work in favour of such a belief. We have seen that through English poetry and German idealism both the relationship between reality and the ideal world and the oneness of the universe had already been part of human consciousness for the last sixty years at least; these beliefs had already found full

---

[*] T. S. Eliot, *Selected Essays* (Faber and Faber, 1932), p. 388.

expression in the poetry and critical writings of Coleridge, Shelley and Hölderlin. In France they had acquired some currency through De Maistre, the Illuminists and the works of Balzac and Nerval. As for synaesthesia or interpenetration of the senses—

> *"Comme de longs échos qui de loin se confondent*
> *... Les parfums, les culeurs et les sons se répondent"*

—it is no more new in literature and in human thought than the correspondence between the real and the unreal; when people talk of seeing red or having a weight on their minds, when Shakespeare describes jealousy as a 'green eyed monster', or when Musset talks of *"l'étoile qui pleure, la fleur qui vole et l'oiseau qui embaume"*, they show that the interpenetration of sensations was part of the process of artistic experience, although not an overt part of artistic consciousness. For that we have to wait for the end of the nineteenth century, which saw with psychology the awakening and the increase of self-consciousness and a more subjective form of knowledge.

But if French poetry was slow in becoming attuned with English poetry, French painting was not; and from Constable to Corot and the Impressionists, or from Turner (a seminal influence in painting) to Géricault, Delacroix and the Pointillists, English and French Romanticism were, in that domain, travelling side by side and a good deal of the way in the wake of Byron. Géricault's *Radeau de la Méduse*, Delacroix's *Massacre de Scio*, or *La Barque de Dante*, combine stark naturalism with imagination, in compositions dominated by the ideals which filled French Romantic poetry and Rousseau's writings, and which can be summed up as a plea for the oppressed and the dispossessed. Delacroix, the greatest painter of the nineteenth century, is also the last of the great masters who did not make of painting an end in itself, as was going to be more and more the case, as he is also the last of the great masters who grappled with great human themes which embody lasting truths, which he explored through the handling of colour, volumes and space on canvas. Delacroix's Byronic disdain of the society of his time contrasted with the attitude of Millet and particularly of Courbet, whose political convictions led him to become probably the first social realist painter, using painting as a means of political redress. His *Enterrement à Ornans* is a perfect example of conceptual naturalism, something which Delacroix, profoundly devoted to imagination, despised, and which he always managed to avoid, even in spite of his enthusiasm for the cause of freedom. *La Liberté guidant le peuple* expresses such an idealistic enthusiasm, without nevertheless falling into naturalistic conceptualism.

After Delacroix, the great experiments in colours carried out by Turner find their continuation and development in the paintings of the Impressionists, who translated reality into impressions of colours, while Cézanne inaugurated his search for the basic geometrical forms of Nature which blossomed into Cubism. The only great artist of the western world who, before the triumph of modern art, sought once more to deal with themes as it had been done by the great masters of the past was Rodin. His masterpiece, *Balzac*, emerging from the elements which his once great imagination transformed, is reminiscent of Michelangelo's *Rondanina Pietà*. Balzac is not Christ, and Rodin is not quite Michelangelo, yet it is obvious that beyond the centuries genius links up with genius in attempts to extract from matter the very meaning of life and creation and, in the case of Michelangelo, the source of the very mystery of the incarnation, and of the continuous travail of matter in order to produce spirit.

The great revolution, which had started in the name of liberty, equality and fraternity, was in the end taken over by the middle class. Nineteenth-century middle class was different from any previous middle class, in the sense that it was a middle class which was part of a disintegrated society. Christ was dead; society had no longer a centre; it had only values which varied according to its various layers, but as the middle class was the dominant element, the dominant values were those of the middle class. These were the values of men, quite pleased with themselves, quite the jingoists, whether they were French, English or German, trusting in the vision and achievement of science to produce greater and greater wealth through industrialization, and looking upon art and poetry not as creations of the imagination, but as a means of adornment and superficial entertainment. In an age of faith, all works of art express the same attitude and have the same function, which is to mediate between man and his Creator. The wealthy and powerful patrons of the art of the Renaissance were part and parcel of an integrated society, and they did not interfere, even in the case of portraiture, with the dialogue between the artist and his Maker. Seventeenth-century society was also fully integrated, and its middle class believed in art values which the artist could express. But once society had disintegrated, the middle class became an end in itself, and as it possessed the greatest buying power, it expected art to conform to its taste. In nineteenth-century France, the middle class or the bourgeoisie, which was without any true Christian values, found itself caught between the rising popular forces of radicalism, on the one side, and, on the other, the dreamers about traditions and past glories which could not be recaptured. Art, for the bourgeois, could not possibly exhibit either reformatory zeal and concern with man's fate or passion for a lost past. The result was that true imagination had nothing to feed on, and was supplemented by fancy which could only produce decoration and titillation for the bourgeois; if these tastes were not met, the bourgeois withheld its purchasing power. Yet the more the bourgeois called for art as decoration, the more the artist rebelled and retreated into the isolation of his group.

The situation was not quite the same in England as in France. The cleavage between the artist and society was much less marked there than in France. Even the savagery with which Oscar Wilde was treated does not add up to the climate of hostility and mutual dislike which existed between the artist and society in France. The truth is that the concept of the bourgeois is something typically French and certainly not English. The Cromwellian revolution, which put an end to absolute monarchy, and the fact that Protestantism took a more active part than Catholicism in political and social life, produced in England a society which, although strongly stratified, was not as deeply cleft into two parts as was French society up to 1789. After the Revolution, in spite of the Napoleonic system of education and system of promotion in the army, both aimed at mixing up the classes and at giving full scope to talent, the French middle class, which was not as well off as the English middle class, developed an ethos of its own, which was basically materialistic and in which religion was either discarded or merely kept as a convenient set of social conventions or appearances and nothing more. The English middle class, less affected by mechanistic materialism and scientism than the French middle class,

107

maintained a kind of religiosity which made itself felt in the arts, and which is well summed up by Matthew Arnold's notion of art as a substitute for religion and for religious feelings. There never was in England any deep animosity between the artist and the middle class, and the pre-Raphaelites and poets like Tennyson met its taste half-way by indulging its fashionable love of legends and of the past, its vicarious love of adventures and exoticism, and its superficial romanticism. In that society Browning sought better climates, and Hopkins, one of its most significant products, remained unknown until the twentieth century.

The problem was much more acute in France, and for the first time in the history of art, artists ended in seeing themselves as a coherent, social group or an entity at war with a society which was blind or totally opposed to their attempts to create the new world that they envisaged. So poets, painters and musicians came together, animated by the same ideals, and they sought to rediscover or to search through art for a new world. Since society was hostile, it was no use working for society and producing images, stories, poems or music that it would understand, appreciate or find satisfaction in. The fine art authorities, the art galleries and the academic world could safely be trusted to meet this demand. So the artists took their own separate way. The painter stopped painting his sitter or some landscape; he painted instead what he himself felt in front of either of them. The poet no longer cared about telling a story, entertaining or trying to interest a society which did not care for him; so he worked only for initiates, and he sought to convey what he felt and what was the result of the confrontation of his subjectivity with the experience of living in his age. It was an experience of revolt, disgust, flight, as in the case of Rimbaud, or of sheer negation of reality and refuge in the transcendentalism of creation, as is the case with Mallarmé. In the past, the artist had never set himself in conflict against society. Villon was a thief and a pimp, Michelangelo refused to obey the Pope, but these delinquencies, quarrels and samples of anti-social behaviour were individual acts. By the end of the nineteenth century, the artist was at war with a society which, in the cases of Flaubert, Baudelaire and Wilde, did not hesitate to exercise harsh reprisals.

X

Modern Times

From the Romantic age onward, art, in a world without religion, has tended to become more and more a faith and a cult in the name of which the artist is prepared to accept martyrdom, isolation and even death. As the world in which he lives is irrational while claiming to be rational, as his world is unfriendly and inhuman, the artist rejects appearances and endeavours to create a world in which the creative act and himself are absolutely self-sufficient in the transcendental act of creation which negates the phenomenal world and replaces it by the creating subject, projected out of reality, as absolute. Great art has always required some kind of transcendence with which the artist tries to connect. The modern artist, conscious of his separation from transcendence, and of his alienation from a society which has no use for him except as entertainer, aims at replacing transcendence by the creative act. From Cézanne to Van Gogh, Rouault, Rimbaud and Mallarmé, the urge to artistic expression is dominated by the belief that what matters is not the world of appearances but the other, the one which the artist creates through his vision, enabling him to discover the essence of being in a bowl of fruit or in writhing olive groves, or to see a ship-wrecked cathedral in the sky or great mysterious wings which carry the poet out of the earth. Great as was the cleavage between the artist and society, or perhaps because of it in this case, this was a great creative age, one of the greatest mankind has ever known. One would think that imagination, deprived of the noble and sublime aims which it had had in the past, cut off from a world which repudiated it, had taken wings to soar upwards in order to create, through this very movement, its own light and its own triumph. Cubism opens up a new age in painting and symbolism in poetry, though not an original venture, but a self-conscious continuation of English Romanticism, from Blake to Coleridge and Shelley, has brought to poetry autonomy and a will to reach or to suggest the mystery of Being, which connects it with the light with which Shakespeare looked at Macbeth and Lear, and Rembrandt at *The Three Crosses.* Poetry passes from a poetry of statement and lucid expression to a poetry of images, symbols, metaphors, music, mystery and vagueness. It no longer describes, it suggests, and is thus creative in the sense that the reader must contribute his own subjectivity. Carlyle and Schopenhauer had already anticipated this aspect of poetry, and Turner's mysterious colours express in paint the same sensibility in search of mystery. This great flowering of the arts continues in the twentieth century and bears, above all, the mark of the French genius which has reached with it one of its peaks. Creativeness seems indeed to proceed mysteriously through subterranean terrain, which can neither be charted nor defined, according to social and economic conditions. Art is not a matter of social prosperity, political stability or harmony between the artist and society. There certainly are enough instances to justify any of these contentions; yet such justification shows the impossibility of establishing any widely valid relationship between any of these aspects of society and the blossoming of art. Victorian England, to take one instance, was both prosperous and politically stable, yet art in it was at a low ebb. Nineteenth- and twentieth-century France was reasonably prosperous, politically unstable, with a fragmented society in search of some political or religious centre and internally at war with itself, yet art reached one of its all-time high watermarks. It seems to me that great art is only achieved in a society which, whatever its shape, is integrated and shares in the sense of the numinous and the sacred or by men who, conscious of the absence of transcendence and of its rejection by society, have in themselves the conviction that their vision of essence and of true being can relate them to transcendence and enable them to contribute to the liberation of their fellow beings from the materialistic society in which they live and from the bonds of Destiny. Picasso, Braque, Matisse, Claudel, Proust, Mauriac, Malraux, Gide and Valéry, epitomize the vitality of artistic creation in modern France. Great Britain caught the impact of this creativity a little later than France, but by the twentieth century,

Yeats, the greatest poet in English since the Romantic age, had found his true voice. He was soon followed by Eliot, Pound and D. H. Lawrence and, in the arts, by Barbara Hepworth, Henry Moore, Ben Nicholson, Sutherland and others, who show that by now the arts and literature of our time move on a European plane and not on a national plane, as before.

In England, the experience of surrealism did not have any effect until the movement had died down, and, in fact, it never found much support in this country. In France, the surrealists, and later anti-social writers like Genet and others, sought to use their writings like dynamite in order to blow up society. So a new type of art has been born which embraces practically the entire world, and this art has turned its back on nature and society because they are both incomprehensible, and because appearance, in a dis-integrated world, has no true reality and is merely an illusion or sham, like the society which believes in it. The entertainer, the artist as decorator, the money-maker will play society's game, and provide the superficial commodity it asks for. This commodity will not be art but decoration, sensualism disguised as art, and vague cerebrations disguised as profundities. Poetry will be pseudo-poetry, vague high-flown forms and images, born from fantasy, but not fused together into a whole by imagination. Billetdoux in France, Shaffer in this country, provide good examples of this psuedo-poetry, which gives self-satisfied audiences the illusion that this is the real thing. These same audiences will find the poetry of Eliot, Pound and Dylan Thomas too abstruse and that of Claudel too demanding and too concentrated to be worth the effort required, in order to try to grasp the truth which it contains. This does not mean that the works of authentic poets like Yeats, Eliot, Claudel, Brecht or O'Neill are totally ignored; but it certainly does mean that, compared with the Beatles, the pop-singers and the T.V. personalities, their influence and presence are practically non-existent. Beckett, with a stroke of genius, produced an image of the human condition entrapped in historical conditions and obsessed by the mystery of its destiny. No sooner had he done that than our mass-producing society seized upon the mechanics of his plays and started to churn out imitations by the dozen.

Because we have just emerged from the most ferocious display of violence the world has ever known, a violence compared with which the world of tigers and lions is angelic, because violence is all around us in open wars, gangsterism and racial battles in the streets of our towns, and because we are dimly afraid of the lurking, apocalyptic, nuclear catastrophy, we are obsessed by violence, and consequently the so-called arts indulge the mimetic fallacy of staging or of representing untransmuted violence, in the belief that it has some therapeutic or cathartic effect and is art. We are given, as an excuse, by incompetent pundits, the example of the Greeks and of Shakespeare. They ignore the fact that the naturalistic representation of violence does not call forth imaginative experience but, purely and simply, kinetic reactions. Violence in art must be submitted to a style and integrated into the imaginative wholeness of the work of art. Aeschylean and Sophoclean Oedipus Rex and Orestes may drip with blood, but the violence of which they are both the instruments and the sufferers has been willed by the Gods, and the lesson or the experience suggested by these characters is that it is man's triumph to achieve, through this ordained violence, forgiveness, justice and the transcendental joy of having overcome Destiny. The violence of Shakespeare is of a similar nature. It is never violence for violence's sake out of sheer pessimism, as some would have it, but as an integral part of poetic justice and of the discovery of truth, which, as Christ crucified and other lesser heroes of mankind have shown, had to suffer violence in order that truth could be known. The distortion and the apparent agony of Grünevald's Christ are not meant to extract from the onlooker a sense of horror, but to strike him to the depth of his being by showing him what the Man-God had to endure to reveal truth and a true sense of vocation to man.

Lear does not go mad, does not provoke and endure the death of his daughter, in order merely to have us shaken out of our wits by watching Gloucester have his eyes put out or the crude brutalities of Goneril and Regan. He endures all to show us, as Shakespeare wonderfully understood it, that the way to illumination, to the light of the cross or of *The Three Crosses* with which Rembrandt placed man face to face with his fate, is through suffering, and through the night which ends with the dawn. Life is, according to Macbeth, "a tale told by an idiot, full of sound and fury, signifying nothing".   But Macbeth's death gives this tale told by an idiot a meaning. The tragedy of Macbeth is, in many ways, like that of Adam the first man, for like him, he is born with all the qualities and possibilities of a good or an evil man. He has courage and nobility; he is admired by his friends and his king, he is loved by his wife, and he is also endowed with the imagination which can project him forward into the great rôle he has to play, that of a great leader of men. At the same time, he has what some great destructive geniuses of mankind, like Tamburlaine or Hitler, did not have—a conscience. He is profoundly aware of evil, as aware of it as Baudelaire, and the more he sinks into it by the sheer law of mathematical progression which applies to evil, the more he is conscience-stricken at the thought that he has irretrievably lost the priceless jewel which is his soul to the enemy of man, and the more he is aware that time cannot be redeemed. Christ, for him, has come and gone, unseen, while he, more and more aware of his unbridgeable separation from God, finds that time creeps on all too slowly for someone who, like him, knows that he is on the threshold of an eternity of suffering.

The tragedy of Macbeth is his growing awareness of his unredeemable crimes. Therefore, it is not what he does that matters, for what is done is done, but what he feels about what has been done. His wife, who like most women only lives in the present and always brings everything, through daydreams and fancy, to the present, is completely fascinated by the glitters of the regal crown and cannot see anything else around it, simply because she has fancy but no imagination. Macbeth, on the other hand, has too much imagination; yet although he has, through it, the power of evil, he requires, in order to proceed to deeds, the proddings of his ambition, which is given concrete evidence through the witches, who confirm the projections of his imagination, and through his wife, who, at the moment when he is caught between imagination and conscience and is about to topple on the side of conscience, stuns him with words and compels him to eat, like Adam, the forbidden fruit, that is to say, to indulge his tormenting appetite for power. Once this is done, God becomes the enemy, and the more Macbeth can do to offend Him and to attract His attention the better. Thence the ruthless murder of Malcolm's children. "See," he cries to God "what you, you who forsook me, have made me do!" and of course he does all that in utter defiance and in the knowledge that he himself is damned. Therefore nothing matters. His wife "should have died hereafter", and he, like Lucifer hurled out of heaven, is prepared to wrestle for eternity on the edge, between the world which he has lost and the world to which he will henceforth belong.

Only those who fail to grasp the fall of Macbeth as his voyage through darkness towards the liberation of death, or those who reduce the universality and wholeness of *King Lear*, the most complex and profound tragedy ever written, to one single slab of dark pessimism and brutality, can invoke Shakespeare as a patron of naturalistic pictures of violence for violence's sake. They ignore the fact that the true artist is always concerned either with the eternal or with what transcends his own selfhood and relates it to permanence, and never with the use of sensations and sensationalism for the listener's or the viewer's delectation. Pop art can do that, but that can no more take the place of art than a will-o'-the-wisp or a fire-fly can take the place of a searchlight or of the rays of the sun. The former is only an instant flash, without past or future, without continuity or prolongation; the latter is an illumination of a whole area of human life, which plunges as far as the eyes can see into the distance, into the past and into the future.

Modern man may not have, as a whole, a sense of the future, though even this proposition becomes doubtful, if one thinks, among others, of the millions of Christians and Marxists, who compose the population of the earth; but the absurdists and the pessimists apart, there is in life a definite sense of destiny that can be reconciled with Christianity and with Marxism, two creeds which imply, each in its own terms, a more or less self-determined finality. On the whole, it can be said that the world is divided into two categories. On the one side there is nihilism, sensualism, sensationalism and absurdism, on the other, Christianity and Marxism together with the two main religions of the Middle East and of the Far East, Islamism and Buddhism. Leaving out of any possible discussion the attributes of the Divinity or the dogmatics of the established churches, what matters is the principle, widely accepted by all those who, church-goers or otherwise, call themselves Christian, that looks upon the individual as part of a whole greater than himself and both sums up and fosters or inspires the best that man can give. Marxism, though it fails to recognize in clear-cut terms the intrinsic value of the individual, nevertheless believes in the perfectibility and ultimate greatness of man. Neither Buddhism nor Islamism is fundamentally concerned with the sacredness of the individual and with the vital notion (source of human endeavours) that Time is the midwife of Eternity, but the needs for the use of western technology and social reforms are making themselves felt in countries which practise these two faiths.

France has a communist party which could poll, at certain moments, over five million votes, and which has become so respectable as to ally itself with the socialist party in order to provide an opposition and, if possible, a government. France, which has gone through the trauma of defeat, occupation and rebellion against the enemy, seems to be now at the tail-end of one of the greatest periods of creativity that mankind has ever known, and she seems to have switched part of her energy towards economic and technological developments. She has shed unwillingly, and through a good deal of political anarchy and mismanagement, an Empire, but she has succeeded, thanks to her late leader's wisdom, in coming to terms with Algeria and in turning former clients into adult friends. Great Britain has shed an Empire, and has found herself exhausted and tired by the war and rather bewildered by her sudden change in status. However adventuresome and thrusting in commerce and colonial expansions she has been since the Victorian age, she has not been very vital in the arts, though this only means that she has not been as vital as France. As the land of pragmatism and experimental rationalism, she has not found it uncongenial to adopt the logical positivism which is a development of these philosophical attitudes. As far as philosophical thought is concerned, France, after Auguste Comte, who had a limited impact, turned towards idealism and metaphysics, and later to existentialism, phenomenalism and structuralism, and it must be said that all these new philosophical experiments have found little echo or sympathy in this land of pragmatism and positivism. This attitude either entails or suggests a lack of faith in imagination and interest for things which are beyond the reach and the range of perceptions and perceptual measurements, and it seems to be reflected in the arts, which, whether in poetry or painting, seem, to a certain extent, to suffer from inhibitions about

115

imagination and a certain self-consciousness which can produce anæmia or self-assertion. This is not the case with the Celtic elements, who are born metaphysicians and have kept faith in imagination and with the emotions: Yeats, Synge, Dylan Thomas, MacDiarmid and, although not belonging to the Celtic element, the passionately earnest and deeply intuitive D. H. Lawrence, connect with the world of metaphysics and imagination of the great Romantics.

At this moment French and English seem to exhibit two slightly different approaches to thought, which are quite conformable to their respective traditions. The French continue their explorations of the mind and the heart with a combination of energy and passion which tends to fuse facts into the kind of structure which the mind anticipates. The English continue to respect the fact, perhaps too much, but that is a debatable point; they move at a steady pace towards a structure, the coping-stone or final shape of which does not seem to trouble them until they have reached it. They will simply see what it is like once the work has been completed or the summit reached. There is a lot to be said for this steadfastness and patience, which precludes intolerance, lack of respect for reality, or violence to it. The French have always been much perturbed by the summit or goal to be reached, and by the idea or the theoretical scheme of things. Valéry loved this notion so much that for him it was the only thing that mattered, and he thought that he could very well spend his working life watching his mind going through the endless permutations of its changing moods and movements, in search of itself, and being itself the movement. From Descartes to Valéry, with a refreshing surge forward in Hegel's philosophy in order to maintain the momentum, we find that in France, the love of, and the faith in, the mind is unbroken. This explains the French scepticism from Montaigne to Valéry, their ceaseless curiosity about all the possibilities of the mind, and the passion with which they grapple with ideas. The English distrust them, as naturally as one distrusts snakes or eels; they are, at times, disquieting and elusive, though they can also be dazzlingly beautiful in the glory of their multi-coloured scales. The whole problem is not to be afraid of them, not to throw stones at them, and then bitterly regret such a gesture, as Lawrence did. The fact is that ideas are both beautiful and ugly, good

116

and bad according to the moment, the time, the place or the priority which one grants them. If one is obsessed by them, to the point of ignoring everything else, including reality, or of wanting to shape the phenomenal world in order to suit them, they become bad influences and dangerous to the equilibrium and the progress which man longs for. But then, of course, they are no longer ideas but ideologies, and the modern world has had quite enough of them, with Nazism, Fascism and Stalinism. But if ideas and ideals are what they ought to be, that is to say, the light which illumines facts, the filigree which underlies them and structures them into artistic entities or political patterns which express the true life of man, then ideas are the glimmers of what is eternal in the human mind and the motivation that makes it one and enables it constantly to move forward towards a more and more luminous future. Whatever atheists may say, whether they follow Sartre or Marx, they have not been able to avoid the notion of a transphenomenal reality, which emerges here and there out of the vast mass of mankind in the same way as will-o'-the-wisps surge from the darkness of night and, for a brief moment, illumine it and point the way.

The English respect ideas and ideals, but neither the Berkeleyan approach to reality nor the Hegelian has ever had much success in England. Reality is approached through sense-data, perceptions and concepts extracted from them. The phenomenal world and the senses are the basis of knowledge. The English may, as Emerson put it, "plough their furrow with their plough hitched to a star", but their feet are solidly on the earth, and in preference to the dreams of tomorrow or the risks of glorious and rewarding stakes, they on the whole opt for stability, steady progress, and the certainty of maintaining what has already been peacefully acquired or achieved. This may be due, as Napoleon caustically remarked, to a shopkeeper mentality. But it is also due to the kind of level-headedness and sense of equilibrium which has made of this country the most politically stable country in the world, and this stability has lasted for centuries. Whatever young agitators, Maoists or others, may hope for, they are certainly wasting their time in England, because the English innate love of stability precludes, unless circumstances alter dramatically, revolutionary fervour, adventurousness and the taking of risks to win new

117

worlds. Most people have already acquired enough well-being to make it difficult for them to gamble it away in adventures. The new Jerusalem is not yet here, but England is nevertheless very far from the Blakean dark mills and Dickensian exploitations, and she is just as far from Mill, Bentham and Cobden with their dreams of free-trade and economic liberalism. The middle class, which includes the workers and is therefore the dominant class, is neither interested in revolution nor in free enterprise, which could endanger its stability. The English are probably the greatest gamblers in the world; they gamble on horses, dogs, electoral polls, etc., but certainly not on political life, sports or other serious matters like war. Cricket is their national game, and cricket is essentially a matter of teamwork. Football and Rugby are also, up to a point, a matter of teamwork, but a France-England rugby match easily illustrates some of the differences between the French and the English. Translating these attitudes and beliefs into socio-political terms, it seems reasonable to say that Hobbesian materialistic naturalism, with its respect for moral rules and the power of the state, its acceptance of man's desire for self-preservation as well as for pleasure, still play an important part in the make-up of the English psyche.

Contemporary French thought has, from Bergson to Sartre, Marcel and Merleau-Ponty, on the whole, broken away from Cartesian conceptualism, and has taken on a subjective, existential stand which relates it to the introspectives and to Pascal. The subject-object distance has been, as in the arts, abolished. It is the same with the notion of sequential time. The analytical process of Descartes, consisting in reducing truth to its component, self-evident elements, has been found wanting, particularly after the Kantian antinomies, his differentiation between practical and pure reason and his rejection of the *cogito*. They have been replaced by the notion that truth is not a matter of analytical reduction to the simplest component elements and to essence, but a matter of relationship and fields of activities to which each individual belongs and by which he is related to other fields, themselves related to a central organic force or principle which holds them together and is the essence or the archetype of the principle which animates the various separate fields and their component elements. This is not a restatement of Monadism; it is a subjective apprehension

118

of truth in conformity with the structural field to which it belongs.

In fact the modern notion of truth could best be summed up by the Husserlian notion of relating the essence of any individual subjectivity to the essence of intersubjectivity; it is therefore not an ascesis of the *I* or subject, but a relating of the *I* or subject to that field or fields to which it belongs. A quotation from Merleau-Ponty about language truly marks the end of conceptualism and advocates the use of language as Plato used it on occasions, and as modern poets try to use it all the time: "The words which are the most laden with philosophy are not necessarily those which are fully laden with meaning. They are rather those which open upon Being, because they convey with greater exactitude the life of the whole and so can cause every day facts to vibrate until they break apart. The question is whether philosophy, and the rediscovery of fundamental or true being, can accomplish its aim through rational language, or if, on the contrary, language should not be shorn of direct and immediate meaning and be used as an equivalence or an entity which suggests what it tries to say." The use of language not as a Cartesian instrument of definition and delineation, but as the means to connect with Being is fundamentally the way of Shakespeare, of Wordsworth, of Shelley and of the great tradition of English poetry to which, since symbolism, French poetry has been attuned.

Although art and philosophy are two aspects of the search for perennial and historical truth, it is as well that art is an independent activity governed by the laws of the imagination and not an imaginative embodiment of truths discovered or suggested by philosophy. If it were not so, French and British art would be as far apart as their respective philosophies. The significance of these respective philosophies as embodiments of social attitudes and sensibility is somewhat difficult to assess. One could be tempted to say that logical positivism, which is the dominant English philosophical creed at the moment, has deep and wide ranging correspondences in English society, even though it has very little in common with its main artists, while, on the contrary, French subjective and objective existentialism, which includes both Catholicism and Marxism, correspond both to the sensibility of France's main artists and to that of wide sections of

French society. The much talked-about structuralism, which in the arts and philosophy is nothing but holism writ large, and the anarchism and activism of the student world are both transient and superficial phases which do not amount to profound and significant groundings in French thought and society.

"Philosophy may in no way interfere with the actual use of language; it can in the end only describe it. For it cannot give it any foundation either. It leaves everything as it is." Thus writes Wittgenstein, who has dominated English philosophy for the last four decades. This philosophy is merely concerned with the technicality and variations of ordinary language, and with language as a self-contained system of verbal games which the philosopher describes and controls. The great problem of western philosophy, the ideas which have moved men's minds since men have begun to think, are totally ignored or dismissed as meaningless because they appear to be mathematically or perceptually unverifiable. The English have always been wary of metaphysics and, to a large extent, of ideas, although of course the philosophies of Locke, Hume, Berkeley and Bradley have not shunned metaphysics, and are part and parcel of the great stream of western philosophy. Logical positivism is, in many ways, a withdrawal from the main current of western thought, or it is perhaps more apt to say that logical positivism is only a very limited aspect of western rationalism. Yet, on the other hand, it is quite conformable to the English love of technicalities, conformism, religiosity, ideas-emotions, and respect for customs and authority, as if change was not the most fundamental aspect of life at all levels. Avoidance of metaphysics, of wide-ranging systems and relationships, and love of techniques are responsible for fragmentation, that is to say, for the lack of a sense of wholeness which relates various human activities around certain key centres, whether religious or political. This is particularly felt in the lower ranges of poetry and of the novel, and in art and literary criticism. The lower ranges of poetry and of the novel which are alluded to are those overconcerned with facts, autobiographical or otherwise, with journalistic topicalities, and with the low-keyed aspects of everyday life. Art and literary criticism are primarily concerned with techniques, and they exhibit little concern for the essence of the work of art and the historical, social, individual causes of evolving and changing styles. Neither the purely linguistic approach nor Leavisian moral asceticism and empiricism can transcend the boundaries of the provincialism and nationalism which these approaches posit.

Still, these attitudes only affect the lower ranges of art, and in the higher reaches, that is to say, the reaches where it is no longer talent or fashion which are at work, but true genius expressing the significant aspects of the sensibility of our time, France and Britain are at one. These geniuses or major artists are Lawrence, Yeats, Eliot, W. H. Auden, Graham Greene, Henry Moore, Barbara Hepworth, Claudel, Valéry, Supervielle, St. John Perse, Eluard, Pierre-Jean Jouve, Pierre Emmanuel, Malraux, Rouault, Picasso, Braque and Matisse, to quote but a few. This sensibility, whether it is profoundly Christian, like that of Eliot, Claudel, Rouault, Simone Weil or Teilhard de Chardin, or unmindful of religion, like that of Valéry and Yeats, can best be described in terms of subjective existentialism. For whether these poets and artists believe in the importance of historical time, as most of them do, or in time as the midwife of Eternity, in both cases the reality of existence can only be tested in time and beaten into lasting gold, or lasting shape, through the pulse of individual life in Time. *"Je vis, je respire, rien de plus"*, said Valéry in *Mon Faust*, and for Eliot, Yeats, Claudel or Bergson, it is only through time lived at the level of intense moments, starting as Yeats put it "in the foul rag-and-bone shop of the heart", that a new terrible beauty connected with, and reflecting, supernal beauty can be born, and that the individual can reach true reality and conquer Time.

Time the destroyer, Time the midwife of Eternity, Time the redeemer, has many facets and has had many meanings. Contemporary time is very different from Cartesian, Hobbesian or Hegelian time of the past centuries. The world is no longer now the materialist world consisting of lumps of matter obeying determined laws perfectly apprehensible to reason. Matter has disintegrated into atoms, protons and neutrons and still smaller particles like electrons whose unpredictable behaviour has opened the door to chance and to statistical probabilities as respectable participants in modern epistemology. Nature and reality have become difficult to define, and they are elusive to the point that one can no longer trust representation or phenomenalism as being able to describe or to convey in any way the mystery of reality which eludes reason. The new philosophy and the new science, including atomic science, have brought about new notions of Time, of which the bulk of mankind may be dimly aware, and which the artist apprehends with certainty and exactness through the imagination, which unites all discoverers of truth whether they are artists or scientists. In 1905, Einstein postulated the equivalence of mass and energy, and proposed the solution of the great problem, which had led Leibnitz, Newton and Clarke to sharp epistolary exchanges and Kant to long and inconclusive meditations, the problem of Space and Time. Einstein proposed the amalgamation of Space and Time into a four dimensional space continuum, the subjective apprehension of which was not far from the Bergsonian duration. Artistic experience had already moved in that direction, and at about the same time the search for the essence of truth, which had led Cézanne to reducing objects to such basic structures as the cylinder and the cube, burst into full self-consciousness with the work of Picasso and Braque.

While in England poetry was still bathing in Georgian rusticity waiting for Yeats to find his voice and for Eliot and Pound to attune it to the new sensibility, art, French art particularly, was becoming more and more non-representational in the face of a less and less comprehensible and disorganized world. Things had fallen apart well before Yeats reported this fact. The self, the solid Cartesian ego, had long ago melted in the Freudian subconscious, and the great intersubjective—God, source of all selves— had disappeared. So any attempt to reach the self could only end in a confrontation with nothingness. Sartre cheerfully tried to strike freedom out of this non-existent, sombre flint. But not everyone could have the same enthusiasm for living nothingness, nor the same joy in forsaking logic. The only reality the artist could be certain of was that of his own creativity. Mallarmé had already blazed the trail. Creativity is, from then on, embodied in unchanging material shapes—lines, colours or words which abstract the world or suggest the artist's inner fluctuations in an unquiet world—through images, parts of a greater image, myths, symbols or legends which suggest the modern predicament. Valéry's *La Jeune Parque*, Eliot's *Waste Land*, Joyce's *Ulysses*, Cubism, analytical or synthetic, are of this nature. Recognizable or not recognizable, phenomenal reality is of no importance; what matters is the way the artist orchestrates his colours and forms; for in his world he can count on nobody but himself. In a different way, tachism, action-painting, abstract expressionism, tell all similar experiences. This great diversity of art forms, and in many cases, of pseudo-art, corresponds to a chaotic, non-integrated, non-purposive world.

There is no question of positing as an ideal the theocentric world of the Middle Ages and of the Renaissance, or the unified and integrated world of Greece. What is past is past. These were moments in the life of mankind when societies were small and hierarchically homogeneous; nowadays a great deal of human living, feeling and thinking takes place on a world scale. The mass media of publicity, television, cinema and the press tend more and more to fashion man's sensibility on a world-wide pattern, and in years to come there will certainly be what might be called an earth ethos as there are now various national ethos, or it might be a television ethos, for television presides over everything—birth, death, elections, games, and every aspect of human life and social expression. In fact, while Mallarmé believed that *"le monde existe pour aboutir à un livre"*, now everything seems to exist purely in order to be material for television, that is to say, in order to be a very ephemeral source of sensations. The great discoverers of truth, in science or in art, are far less important than the various stars of television and screen. Notoriety and economic reward are the greatest criteria of value of our age. The result of all this is vulgarization, greater concern for appearance than for substance, pandering to the taste of the masses, egalitarianism so as not to offend these masses, and adoption of the fashions and attitudes of the day, pop music, drugs, anti-racialist agitation, etc., so as to be 'with it'. The corollary to these attitudes is lack of regard for intellectual and moral integrity, for humility, and for devotion and exertions required in order to sustain the quest for truth. This quest will not stop, but our age makes it hard, and I have no doubt that it will be so as long as life, political or religious, whatever the faith, lacks the transcendental dimension necessary for organic integration.

The loom upon which French and English thought and sensibility have been woven has produced, all in all, the most varied and wide-ranging tapestry of art the world has known, and something so complex, so organically interwoven, that it is very difficult to be dogmatic and precise about it. On the one side, Pascal with his *raison du coeur* answers Descartes, in the same way as Claudel answers Valéry, and between the two they exemplify the dialectical strains which are the main component elements of French sensibility. On the other, Coleridge had not only a great imagination, he also had an intrinsically great mind, and he exhibits the organic blend of mind and imagination which to me is the main aspect of the English genius. Eliot had a mind which Valéry would have respected. Blake holds hands with Victor Hugo; Turner and Constable herald the Impressionists; Proust is closer to James Joyce and Virginia Woolf than he is to Gide or to Mauriac; Supervielle's gentle pantheism and fantasy are closer to the English than to the French genius, and, at this moment, Beckett stands squarely astride both. He has the humour, the grasp of facts and wry pathos which are both English and Irish, and he has the intellectual curiosity and the sense of style which are both French and Celtic. He is, as much as any living artist can be, typical of the interpenetration of Franco-British culture. On the other hand, typically English though he was, nobody has contributed more than Locke to French culture. It is evident that, either through complementariness or through interpenetration, French and British cultures throughout the centuries have unfolded as a pattern from which it is not possible to completely unravel any thread without disrupting the whole. Therefore, it seems to me that one could not find a more fitting ending to this brief exploration of our similarities and differences than a quotation from Kipling's poem, part of which has been quoted at the beginning of this essay:

"What can Blood and Iron make more than we have made?
We have learned by keenest use to know each other's mind.
What shall Blood and Iron loose that we cannot bind?
We who swept each other's coast, sacked each other's home,
Since the sword of Brennus clashed on the scales at Rome,
Listen, count and close again, wheeling girth to girth,
In the linked and steadfast guard set for peace on earth!"[*]

[*] Rudyard Kipling, *France 1913*.

Index

Index

Index